Farm To Fork Food Evolution

Farm To Fork Food Evolution

Alina Hazel

UNIEK ENTERPRISES

CONTENTS

INDEX

Chapter 1

Introduction to Farm to Fork

The idea of "Ranch to Fork" has acquired monstrous prevalence lately, reshaping the manner in which we contemplate the food we eat. It is an all encompassing way to deal with food creation and dispersion that spotlights on straightforwardness, supportability, and the excursion of food from its source to our plates. In this paper, we will investigate the Homestead to Fork development, its beginnings, standards, and its effect on the worldwide food framework.

Ranch to Fork, frequently alluded to as "F2F," addresses a takeoff from the customary, frequently murky, and complex food inventory network. It puts a huge accentuation on nearby, natural, and earth mindful cultivating works on, meaning to decrease the carbon impression related with food creation and transportation. Basically, it tries to make an immediate association among ranchers and purchasers, wiping out go-betweens and expanding customer mindfulness about the beginning and nature of their food.

One of the essential main thrusts behind the Ranch to Fork development is the developing worry over the ecological and wellbeing ramifications of our ongoing food frameworks. The industrialization of horticulture has prompted expanded utilization of engineered synthetic substances, monoculture cultivating, and the exhaustion of regular assets. This has brought about soil debasement, water contamination, and a deficiency of biodiversity. Also, the significant distances food goes to arrive at our plates add to ozone depleting substance outflows, further fueling environmental change.

Ranch to Fork looks to alleviate these issues by upholding for reasonable horticulture rehearses. It energizes the utilization of natural cultivating techniques that focus on soil wellbeing and biodiversity. This advances the prosperity of both the climate and the actual ranchers. By shortening the distance among creation and utilization, it lessens the fossil fuel byproducts related with transportation. Purchasers, thusly, benefit from fresher, more nutritious, and more secure food.

The Ranch to Fork development is established in a bunch of center rules that guide its practices and objectives. These standards include:

Nearby Obtaining: F2F advances obtaining food locally whenever the situation allows. This not just backings limited scope ranchers and nearby economies yet in addition decreases the carbon impression of transportation.

Feasible Horticulture: The development energizes reasonable cultivating rehearses that focus on soil wellbeing, lessen synthetic sources of info, and advance biodiversity.

Straightforwardness: Straightforwardness in the food production network is a foundation of Ranch to Fork. Customers reserve the privilege to know where their food comes from and the way things are delivered.

Occasional Eating: F2F accentuates the utilization of occasional and locally accessible produce, decreasing the requirement for energy-concentrated nursery development and significant distance transportation.

Diminished Food Squander: By making a more straightforward association among makers and customers, Ranch to Fork plans to decrease food squander, as there is less deterioration and misfortune along the store network.

Fair Estimating: Ranchers are in many cases come up short on in the traditional food framework. Ranch to Fork advocates for fair evaluating that guarantees ranchers get a sensible portion of the benefits.

Dietary benefit: F2F underlines the nourishing nature of food by advancing practices that keep up with the supplement content of produce.

Food handling: The development additionally focuses on food handling, guaranteeing that buyers approach food that is liberated from destructive pollutants and microorganisms.

Local area Building: Homestead to Fork reinforces the feeling of local area by carrying individuals nearer to the wellspring of their food and encouraging associations among ranchers and shoppers.

Training: One of the vital objectives of F2F is to instruct shoppers about the food they eat, the way things are created, and the effect of their decisions on the climate and their wellbeing.

The Homestead to Fork development has its underlying foundations in different verifiable and social practices. In numerous ways, it draws motivation from conventional and native food frameworks that have existed for quite a long time. These frameworks were portrayed by nearby obtaining, irregularity, and a profound association among networks and the land they occupied. With the appearance of industrialization and globalization, these practices were in many cases minimized for huge scope, benefit driven farming.

Nonetheless, the Homestead to Fork development has seen a resurgence in late many years, driven by the rising consciousness of the weaknesses of the traditional food framework. This resurgence is likewise powered by a longing for better and more manageable food choices. Individuals are progressively worried about the drawn out effect of modern farming on their wellbeing and the climate, and accordingly, they are looking for choices.

One of the trailblazers of the cutting edge Homestead to Fork development is Alice Waters, the famous culinary specialist and pioneer behind Chez Panisse eatery in Berkeley, California. Waters is serious areas of strength for a for privately obtained, natural, and occasional fixings. Her eatery, which opened in 1971, assumed a urgent part in promoting the possibility of "California food" that depended on new, nearby produce. Waters' impact reached out past her café, as she established the Consumable Schoolyard Venture, a drive pointed toward showing youngsters food, cultivating, and sustenance. Her work has motivated endless people and networks to embrace the Homestead to Fork reasoning.

Notwithstanding people like Alice Waters, different associations and drives have arisen to advance and support the Homestead to Fork development. These incorporate ranchers' business sectors, local area upheld horticulture (CSA) projects, and food cooperatives. Ranchers' business sectors give an immediate connection among ranchers and customers, permitting individuals to buy new, neighborhood produce and high quality items. CSA programs empower people to buy into a ranch's occasional collect ahead of time, offering monetary help to ranchers and guaranteeing a stock of new, privately developed food. Food cooperatives are part claimed supermarkets that attention on offering nearby and manageable items.

The European Association (EU) has likewise embraced the Ranch to Fork idea, making it a focal part of the European Green Arrangement. The European Homestead to Fork Procedure, sent off in 2020, plans to change the EU's food framework into an additional supportable and versatile model. It sets aggressive focuses for lessening pesticide use, expanding natural cultivating, and further developing food marking. The EU Homestead to Fork Technique lines up with the Unified Countries' Practical Improvement Objectives, especially Objective 2, which intends to end hunger, accomplish food security, and advance reasonable agribusiness.

The Ranch to Fork development has affected food creation and dispersion as well as reshaped the café business. Numerous cooks and restaurateurs have embraced the standards of F2F, underlining the utilization of privately obtained, supportable fixings in their menus. The homestead to-table development, as it is known in the eatery world, has built up forward momentum, with culinary experts like Dan Stylist and Sean Brock advocating the reason. These culinary pioneers have shown that it is feasible to make remarkable eating encounters while supporting nearby ranchers and advancing economical agribusiness.

One of the eminent parts of the Ranch to Fork development is its flexibility to different social and geological settings. While the standards stay predictable, the particular practices and provokes can shift starting with one locale then onto the next. In certain areas, the development centers around restoring customary cultivating and culinary practices, while in others, it means to address present day difficulties, for example, metropolitan food deserts and the deficiency of agrarian biodiversity.

Ranch to Fork has additionally acquired unmistakable quality in metropolitan regions where admittance to new, privately developed food can be restricted. Metropolitan cultivating, local area nurseries, and roof gardens have become basic pieces of the development. These drives permit city occupants to take part in food creation and reconnect with the wellspring of their food. Furthermore, metropolitan farming lessens the carbon impression related with shipping food from rustic regions to urban communities.

The effect of the Ranch to Fork development reaches out past the quick advantages of better, more feasible food. It has more extensive ramifications for general wellbeing, ecological protection, and financial turn of events. How about we dig into these areas and investigate the multi-layered impacts of F2F.

General Wellbeing:

Homestead to Fork straightforwardly affects general wellbeing by advancing the utilization of new, privately obtained, and occasionally fitting food varieties. This approach urges individuals to eat a more fluctuated diet that lines up with the regular rhythms of the seasons. Thus, people are bound to consume a more extensive scope of leafy foods, which are plentiful in fundamental nutrients, minerals, and cell reinforcements. This can assist with combatting diet-related medical problems like corpulence, coronary illness, and diabetes.

By lessening the utilization of engineered pesticides and compound manures, the development additionally adds to diminishing the openness of customers to possibly unsafe synthetic substances. This is especially huge given the developing worry over the drawn out wellbeing impacts of pesticide buildups on produce.

Furthermore, F2F's accentuation on sanitation and straightforwardness guarantees that buyers approach data about the beginning and creation strategies for the food they eat. This empowers them to pursue informed decisions and keep away from items that might present wellbeing gambles.

Natural Preservation:

The Ranch to Fork development assumes an essential part in ecological preservation. Regular agribusiness rehearses frequently lead to soil debasement, loss of biodiversity, and contamination of streams. Interestingly, F2F supports economical agribusiness rehearses that focus on soil wellbeing and decrease the requirement for substance inputs.

The development advances natural cultivating strategies that kill or altogether decrease the utilization of manufactured .

1.1 Definition and concept of Farm to Fork

The idea of "Homestead to Fork" (F2F) is an exhaustive and groundbreaking way to deal with food creation and dissemination that has picked up huge speed lately. This idea addresses a central change by they way we ponder the excursion of food from its source to our plates, and it includes many standards and practices pointed toward improving the maintainability, straightforwardness, and generally speaking nature of our food frameworks.

At its center, Homestead to Fork is about restoring an immediate and straightforward association between food makers, like ranchers and anglers, and buyers. It looks to overcome any barrier between the beginning of our food and the finish of its excursion on our plates. Thusly, it puts areas of strength for an on nearby and local food frameworks, supportability, and moral contemplations, which influence the climate as well as general wellbeing and the prosperity of networks.

The Homestead to Fork idea advances a large group of rules that shape its primary way of thinking. These standards guide the development and highlight its targets:

Neighborhood Obtaining: Ranch to Fork empowers the obtaining of food from nearby and local makers whenever the situation allows. This supports nearby economies as well as diminishes the carbon impression related with moving food over significant distances.

Practical Farming: Manageability is a focal precept of the F2F development. It advances cultivating rehearses that focus on the strength of the dirt, decrease the utilization of manufactured synthetic compounds, and improve biodiversity. Practical agribusiness means to shield regular assets for people in the future.

Straightforwardness: Straightforwardness in the food store network is fundamental in Ranch to Fork. Customers reserve the option to know where their food comes from, the way things are delivered, and the excursion it takes prior to arriving at their plates. This enables people to go with informed decisions about what they eat.

Occasional Eating: F2F advocates for the utilization of food that is in-season and locally accessible. This diminishes the requirement for energy-concentrated nursery development and significant distance transportation, adjusting utilization to regular developing cycles.

Diminished Food Squander: By shortening the distance among makers and purchasers, the Ranch to Fork development decreases food squander along the store network. Fresher, privately obtained food is less inclined to ruin or go to squander.

Fair Evaluating: Ranchers frequently face monetary difficulties in the regular food framework, with many being come up short on for their produce. Ranch to Fork calls for fair evaluating that guarantees ranchers get a simply portion of the benefits, supporting their occupations.

Dietary benefit: F2F underlines the significance of keeping up with the dietary benefit of food. By advancing reasonable cultivating rehearses, it looks to protect the supplement content of produce, bringing about more nutritious nourishment for buyers.

Sanitation: Guaranteeing food handling is a foundation of the Ranch to Fork idea. It requests thorough norms for food handling and quality, furnishing customers with certainty that the food they eat is liberated from destructive pollutants.

Local area Building: F2F cultivates a feeling of local area by carrying individuals nearer to the wellspring of their food. It energizes direct connections among ranchers and buyers, reinforcing the associations that support nearby food frameworks.

Instruction: One of the focal objectives of the Ranch to Fork development is to teach shoppers about the food they eat. It means to expand familiarity with how food is delivered, its effect on the climate, and the advantages of pursuing reasonable and moral decisions.

The Ranch to Fork development finds establishes in different verifiable and social practices have existed for a really long time. In numerous ways, it draws motivation from customary and native food frameworks that were portrayed by nearby obtaining, irregularity, and a profound association among networks and the land they possessed. These frameworks put areas of strength for an on independence and an all encompassing way to deal with food creation.

Over the long run, the appearance of industrialization and globalization prompted the centralization and industrialization of food creation. This brought about enormous scope monoculture cultivating, broad utilization of engineered synthetics, and the exhaustion of normal assets. These practices have prompted huge difficulties, like soil debasement, water contamination, and loss of biodiversity. Moreover, the tremendous distances food goes to arrive at purchasers add to ozone harming substance emanations and intensify environmental change.

The resurgence of the Ranch to Fork development in ongoing many years is, in numerous ways, a reaction to the weaknesses of the traditional food framework. It addresses a developing consciousness of the ecological and wellbeing ramifications of our food decisions. Individuals are turning out to be progressively worried about the drawn out effect of modern farming on their wellbeing and the climate, and they are looking for choices that line up with their qualities.

One of the trailblazers of the cutting edge Ranch to Fork development is Alice Waters, a famous culinary expert and the organizer behind Chez Panisse café in Berkeley, California. Waters is areas of strength for a for privately obtained, natural, and occasional fixings. Her eatery, which opened in 1971, assumed a urgent part in promoting the possibility of "California food" that depended on new, nearby produce. Waters' impact stretched out past her eatery; she established the Consumable Schoolyard Task, a drive pointed toward showing youngsters food, planting, and sustenance. Her work has propelled incalculable people and networks to embrace the Ranch to Fork reasoning.

Notwithstanding people like Alice Waters, different associations and drives have arisen to advance and support the Ranch to Fork development. These incorporate ranchers' business sectors, local area upheld farming (CSA) projects, and food cooperatives. Ranchers' business sectors give an immediate connection among ranchers and buyers, permitting individuals to buy new, neighborhood produce and high quality items. CSA programs empower people to buy into a ranch's occasional collect ahead of time, offering monetary help to ranchers and guaranteeing a stockpile of new, privately developed food. Food cooperatives are part possessed supermarkets that emphasis on offering nearby and practical items.

The European Association (EU) has likewise embraced the Ranch to Fork idea, making it a focal part of the European Green Arrangement. The European Homestead to Fork Procedure, sent off in 2020, means to change the EU's food framework into an additional maintainable and versatile model. It sets aggressive focuses for lessening pesticide use, expanding natural cultivating, and further developing food marking. The EU Ranch to Fork Procedure lines up with the Assembled Countries' Manageable Advancement Objectives, especially Objective 2, which intends to end hunger, accomplish food security, and advance economical agribusiness.

The Homestead to Fork development has impacted food creation and dissemination as well as reshaped the eatery business. Numerous cooks and restaurateurs have embraced the standards of F2F, accentuating the utilization of privately obtained, supportable fixings in their menus. The ranch to-table development, as it is known in the eatery world, has built up some decent forward movement, with gourmet experts like Dan Stylist and Sean Brock advocating the reason. These culinary pioneers have shown that it is feasible to make uncommon eating encounters while supporting neighborhood ranchers and advancing practical horticulture.

One of the eminent parts of the Homestead to Fork development is its flexibility to different social and geological settings. While the standards stay steady, the particular practices and provokes can fluctuate starting with one locale then onto the next. In certain areas, the development centers around restoring conventional cultivating and culinary practices, while in others, it plans to address present day difficulties, for example, metropolitan food deserts and the deficiency of horticultural biodiversity.

Ranch to Fork has additionally acquired unmistakable quality in metropolitan regions where admittance to new, privately developed food can be restricted. Metropolitan cultivating, local area nurseries, and roof gardens have become fundamental pieces of the development. These drives permit city occupants to partake in food creation and reconnect with the wellspring of their food. Also, metropolitan agribusiness diminishes the carbon impression related with shipping food from rustic regions to urban areas.

The effect of the Ranch to Fork development reaches out past the prompt advantages of better, more reasonable food. It has more extensive ramifications for general wellbeing, ecological preservation, financial turn of events, and food security. How about we dive into these areas and investigate the complex impacts of F2F.

General Wellbeing:

Ranch to Fork straightforwardly affects general wellbeing by advancing the utilization of new, privately obtained, and occasionally proper food sources. This approach urges individuals to eat a more shifted diet that lines up with the regular rhythms of the seasons. Therefore, people are bound to consume a more extensive scope of products of the soil, which are plentiful in fundamental nutrients, minerals, and cell reinforcements. This can assist with combatting diet-related medical problems like weight, coronary illness, and diabetes.

By lessening the utilization of engineered pesticides and substance composts, the development likewise adds to diminishing the openness of customers to possibly destructive synthetic compounds. This is especially critical given the developing worry over the drawn out wellbeing impacts of pesticide buildups on produce.

Also, F2F's accentuation on sanitation and straightforwardness guarantees that purchasers approach data about the beginning and creation strategies for the food they eat. This empowers them to settle on informed decisions and keep away from items that might present wellbeing chances.

1.2 Historical perspective of the food industry

The idea of "Homestead to Fork" (F2F) is an exhaustive and groundbreaking way to deal with food creation and dissemination that has picked up huge speed lately. This idea addresses a central change by they way we ponder the excursion of food from its source to our plates, and it includes many standards and practices pointed toward improving the maintainability, straightforwardness, and generally speaking nature of our food frameworks.

At its center, Homestead to Fork is about restoring an immediate and straightforward association between food makers, like ranchers and anglers, and buyers. It looks to overcome any barrier between the beginning of our food and the finish of its excursion on our plates. Thusly, it puts areas of strength for an on nearby and local food frameworks, supportability, and moral contemplations, which influence the climate as well as general wellbeing and the prosperity of networks.

The Homestead to Fork idea advances a large group of rules that shape its primary way of thinking. These standards guide the development and highlight its targets:

Neighborhood Obtaining: Ranch to Fork empowers the obtaining of food from nearby and local makers whenever the situation allows. This supports nearby economies as well as diminishes the carbon impression related with moving food over significant distances.

Practical Farming: Manageability is a focal precept of the F2F development. It advances cultivating rehearses that focus on the strength of the dirt, decrease the utilization of manufactured synthetic compounds, and improve biodiversity. Practical agribusiness means to shield regular assets for people in the future.

Straightforwardness: Straightforwardness in the food store network is fundamental in Ranch to Fork. Customers reserve the option to know where their food comes from, the way things are delivered, and the excursion it takes prior to arriving at their plates. This enables people to go with informed decisions about what they eat.

Occasional Eating: F2F advocates for the utilization of food that is in-season and locally accessible. This diminishes the requirement for energy-concentrated nursery development and significant distance transportation, adjusting utilization to regular developing cycles.

Diminished Food Squander: By shortening the distance among makers and purchasers, the Ranch to Fork development decreases food squander along the store network. Fresher, privately obtained food is less inclined to ruin or go to squander.

Fair Evaluating: Ranchers frequently face monetary difficulties in the regular food framework, with many being come up short on for their produce. Ranch to Fork calls for fair evaluating that guarantees ranchers get a simply portion of the benefits, supporting their occupations.

Dietary benefit: F2F underlines the significance of keeping up with the dietary benefit of food. By advancing reasonable cultivating rehearses, it looks to protect the supplement content of produce, bringing about more nutritious nourishment for buyers.

Sanitation: Guaranteeing food handling is a foundation of the Ranch to Fork idea. It requests thorough norms for food handling and quality, furnishing customers with certainty that the food they eat is liberated from destructive pollutants.

Local area Building: F2F cultivates a feeling of local area by carrying individuals nearer to the wellspring of their food. It energizes direct connections among ranchers and buyers, reinforcing the associations that support nearby food frameworks.

Instruction: One of the focal objectives of the Ranch to Fork development is to teach shoppers about the food they eat. It means to expand familiarity with how food is delivered, its effect on the climate, and the advantages of pursuing reasonable and moral decisions.

The Ranch to Fork development finds establishes in different verifiable and social practices have existed for a really long time. In numerous ways, it draws motivation from customary and native food frameworks that were portrayed by nearby obtaining, irregularity, and a profound association among networks and the land they possessed. These frameworks put areas of strength for an on independence and an all encompassing way to deal with food creation.

Over the long run, the appearance of industrialization and globalization prompted the centralization and industrialization of food creation. This brought about enormous scope monoculture cultivating, broad utilization of engineered synthetics, and the exhaustion of normal assets. These practices have prompted huge difficulties, like soil debasement, water contamination, and loss of biodiversity. Moreover, the tremendous distances food goes to arrive at purchasers add to ozone harming substance emanations and intensify environmental change.

The resurgence of the Ranch to Fork development in ongoing many years is, in numerous ways, a reaction to the weaknesses of the traditional food framework. It addresses a developing consciousness of the ecological and wellbeing ramifications of our food decisions. Individuals are turning out to be progressively worried about the drawn out effect of modern farming on their wellbeing and the climate, and they are looking for choices that line up with their qualities.

One of the trailblazers of the cutting edge Ranch to Fork development is Alice Waters, a famous culinary expert and the organizer behind Chez Panisse café in Berkeley, California. Waters is areas of strength for a for privately obtained, natural, and occasional fixings. Her eatery, which opened in 1971, assumed a urgent part in promoting the possibility of "California food" that depended on new, nearby produce. Waters' impact stretched out past her eatery; she established the Consumable School-yard Task, a drive pointed toward showing youngsters food, planting, and sustenance. Her work has propelled incalculable people and networks to embrace the Ranch to Fork reasoning.

Notwithstanding people like Alice Waters, different associations and drives have arisen to advance and support the Ranch to Fork development. These incorporate ranchers' business sectors, local area upheld farming (CSA) projects, and food co-operatives. Ranchers' business sectors give an immediate connection among ranchers and buyers, permitting individuals to buy new, neighborhood produce and high quality items. CSA programs empower people to buy into a ranch's occasional collect ahead of time, offering monetary help to ranchers and guaranteeing a stockpile of new, privately developed food. Food cooperatives are part possessed supermarkets that emphasis on offering nearby and practical items.

The European Association (EU) has likewise embraced the Ranch to Fork idea, making it a focal part of the European Green Arrangement. The European Home-stead to Fork Procedure, sent off in 2020, means to change the EU's food framework into an additional maintainable and versatile model. It sets aggressive focuses for lessening pesticide use, expanding natural cultivating, and further developing food marking. The EU Ranch to Fork Procedure lines up with the Assembled Countries' Manageable Advancement Objectives, especially Objective 2, which intends to end hunger, accomplish food security, and advance economical agribusiness.

The Homestead to Fork development has impacted food creation and dissemina-tion as well as reshaped the eatery business. Numerous cooks and restaurateurs have embraced the standards of F2F, accentuating the utilization of privately obtained, supportable fixings in their menus. The ranch to-table development, as it is known in the eatery world, has built up some decent forward movement, with gourmet experts like Dan Stylist and Sean Brock advocating the reason. These culinary pioneers have shown that it is feasible to make uncommon eating encounters while supporting neighborhood ranchers and advancing practical horticulture.

One of the eminent parts of the Homestead to Fork development is its flexibility to different social and geological settings. While the standards stay steady, the particular practices and provokes can fluctuate starting with one locale then onto the next. In certain areas, the development centers around restoring conventional cultivating and culinary practices, while in others, it plans to address present day difficulties, for example, metropolitan food deserts and the deficiency of horticultural biodiversity.

Ranch to Fork has additionally acquired unmistakable quality in metropolitan regions where admittance to new, privately developed food can be restricted. Metropolitan cultivating, local area nurseries, and roof gardens have become fundamental pieces of the development. These drives permit city occupants to partake in food creation and reconnect with the wellspring of their food. Also, metropolitan agribusiness diminishes the carbon impression related with shipping food from rustic regions to urban areas.

The effect of the Ranch to Fork development reaches out past the prompt advantages of better, more reasonable food. It has more extensive ramifications for general wellbeing, ecological preservation, financial turn of events, and food security. How about we dive into these areas and investigate the complex impacts of F2F.

General Wellbeing:

Ranch to Fork straightforwardly affects general wellbeing by advancing the utilization of new, privately obtained, and occasionally proper food sources. This approach urges individuals to eat a more shifted diet that lines up with the regular rhythms of the seasons. Therefore, people are bound to consume a more extensive scope of products of the soil, which are plentiful in fundamental nutrients, minerals, and cell reinforcements. This can assist with combatting diet-related medical problems like weight, coronary illness, and diabetes.

By lessening the utilization of engineered pesticides and substance composts, the development likewise adds to diminishing the openness of customers to possibly destructive synthetic compounds. This is especially critical given the developing worry over the drawn out wellbeing impacts of pesticide buildups on produce.

Also, F2F's accentuation on sanitation and straightforwardness guarantees that purchasers approach data about the beginning and creation strategies for the food they eat. This empowers them to settle on informed decisions and keep away from items that might present wellbeing chances.

1.3 The need for a transformative approach

The requirement for an extraordinary methodology in tending to probably the most squeezing difficulties confronting our present reality has never been more critical. From the developing dangers of environmental change and ecological debasement to worldwide food security issues and social disparities, a change in perspective is fundamental to make a more reasonable, impartial, and versatile future. This extraordinary methodology rises above simple steady changes and requires an exhaustive reconsidering of our frameworks, ways of behaving, and esteems. It perceives the interconnected idea of the difficulties we face and looks for inventive arrangements that can address these difficulties all the while.

1. **Environmental Change and Ecological Debasement:**
   Environmental change is a worldwide emergency that requests an extraordinary reaction. The effect of environmental change, including increasing temperatures, outrageous climate occasions, and ocean level ascent, represents an extreme danger to biological systems, economies, and social orders around the world. In addition, natural corruption, from deforestation to soil disintegration, intensifies these issues. Tending to environmental change and ecological debasement requires a key shift away from non-renewable energy sources, impractical land use practices, and asset consumption. Changing to sustainable power sources, embracing regenerative agribusiness, and securing and reestablishing environments are vital stages toward alleviating these difficulties.

2. **Food Security and Supportable Farming:**
   Guaranteeing worldwide food security is another basic test that requires an extraordinary methodology. As the total populace keeps on developing, we should track down ways of creating more food without draining normal assets and intensifying environmental change. Supportable agribusiness rehearses, for example, agroecology and natural cultivating, focus on soil wellbeing, lessen the utilization of manufactured synthetic substances, and advance biodiversity. These methodologies support long haul food security and upgrade the flexibility of food frameworks. Nearby obtaining and the Homestead to Fork development assume fundamental parts in making a more impartial and reasonable food production network, lessening the carbon impression related with food transportation and supporting neighborhood economies.

3. **Wellbeing and Prosperity:**
   The requirement for an extraordinary methodology reaches out to general wellbeing. The ascent of non-transferable infections, like corpulence, coronary illness, and diabetes, is firmly connected to dietary decisions and stationary ways of life. A shift toward a more wellbeing focused approach includes rethinking our food frameworks to focus on new, privately obtained, and healthfully rich food sources. This methodology, combined with an accentuation on actual work and mental prosperity, can significantly affect general wellbeing, lessening the weight of preventable infections and improving by and large prosperity.

4. **Social Imbalances and Value:**
   Extraordinary change is crucial for address social disparities and advance value. Across the globe, variations in pay, admittance to schooling, and medical services continue. To make a more pleasant and all the more society, we want to reexamine our frameworks and strategies. This incorporates carrying out moderate tax assessment, giving admittance to quality training and medical services for all, and tending to foundational predispositions and separation. Engaging underestimated networks and guaranteeing their voices are heard is additionally integral to encouraging social value.

5. **Biodiversity and Preservation:**
   The deficiency of biodiversity and the debasement of normal environments are squeezing concerns. Biodiversity is fundamental for the solidness and flexibility of biological systems and for the arrangement of environment administrations, including fertilization, water filtration, and environment guideline. An extraordinary methodology includes moderating existing biodiversity as well as reestablishing and improving it. Endeavors to safeguard regular living spaces, rewild scenes, and once again introduce cornerstone species can assume an essential part in supporting biodiversity and environment wellbeing.

6. **Round Economy and Feasible Utilization:**
   The direct model of take, make, and discard assets is at this point not valid in that frame of mind with limited assets and mounting waste. A round economy, which centers around diminishing, reusing, and reusing materials, is an extraordinary answer for the difficulties of asset shortage and waste administration. This approach limits the natural effect of utilization and creation while at the same time advancing monetary development and occupation creation.

7. **Mechanical Headways and Advancement:**
   Headways in innovation and advancement are basic to driving groundbreaking change. These advancements range from sustainable power innovations and carbon catch and capacity to leap forwards in biotechnology and man-made consciousness. Innovation can likewise empower more prominent admittance to instruction, medical services, and data, assisting with crossing over cultural imbalances.

8. **Green Money and Speculation:**
   Extraordinary change requires critical ventures and funding. Green money, which channels assets into maintainable and harmless to the ecosystem projects, assumes a basic part in tending to environmental change and natural debasement. This approach advances interest in environmentally friendly power, feasible agribusiness, and protection endeavors.

9. **Schooling and Public Mindfulness:**
   Instructing the general population and bringing issues to light about the requirement for extraordinary change are crucial. This incorporates cultivating a comprehension of the interconnectedness of worldwide moves and enabling people to make a move. Training, both formal and casual, can prompt informed decisions and ways of behaving that help maintainability and versatility.

10. **Worldwide Participation and Administration:**
    Worldwide difficulties require global collaboration and powerful administration. Tending to environmental change, for example, requires multilateral arrangements and deliberate endeavors by countries. Worldwide associations and strategic drives can assume a crucial part in molding worldwide reactions to major problems.

11. **Moral and Values-Based Approaches:**
    An extraordinary methodology ought to likewise think about morals and values. The quest for a more maintainable, fair, and versatile future ought to be directed by standards of obligation, sympathy, and civil rights. Moral contemplations, like regard for the freedoms of people in the future and the characteristic worth of nature, can illuminate our choices and activities.

12. **Strength and Variation:**
    In a world set apart by vulnerability and fast change, it is critical to construct flexibility and versatile limit. Whether it be notwithstanding catastrophic events, financial shocks, or general wellbeing emergencies, versatility is fundamental. This includes planning for and answering emergencies as well as making long haul interests in framework, medical services, and social security nets.

13. **Strengthening and Local area Commitment:**
    Enabling people and networks to be dynamic members in groundbreaking change is crucial. Individuals ought to be participated in dynamic cycles and possess the ability to shape their own predeterminations. Local area driven drives and grassroots developments are many times impetuses for extraordinary change.

14. **Regenerative and Comprehensive Methodologies:**
    An extraordinary methodology ought to be regenerative and comprehensive. This implies recovering normal frameworks, reestablishing harmed biological systems, and taking on a more comprehensive viewpoint that thinks about the interchange of social, natural, and financial variables. Regenerative farming, for instance, encourages soil wellbeing and advances practical land the executives.

15. **Versatile Administration and Strategy Adaptability:**

Strategies and administration designs ought to be versatile and adaptable to address developing difficulties. They ought to consolidate criticism components and the ability to change because of new data and evolving conditions.

Chapter 2

The Sustainable Food Movement

The Practical Food Development is a worldwide peculiarity that has picked up critical speed as of late, determined by a developing consciousness of the natural, social, and wellbeing effects of our ongoing food framework. This development addresses a change in the manner we produce, disperse, and devour food, with an emphasis on manageability, morals, and wellbeing. It envelops many practices and drives pointed toward tending to the complicated difficulties confronting our food framework.

One of the critical mainstays of the Manageable Food Development is the advancement of feasible horticulture. Conventional rural practices have frequently depended on escalated synthetic data sources, monocropping, and unreasonable land the board, prompting soil debasement, water contamination, and loss of biodiversity. Practical horticulture, then again, focuses on natural cultivating strategies, crop turn, and the utilization of regular composts and vermin control techniques to keep up with solid soils and diminish the ecological effect of cultivating.

Neighborhood and limited scope cultivating is one more significant part of the development. Neighborhood food frameworks are intended to diminish the carbon impression of food creation and conveyance by limiting transportation distances. They likewise encourage a feeling of local area and backing nearby economies. Limited scope ranchers are frequently at the very front of manageable food creation, utilizing natural practices, and focusing on moral treatment of animals and fair work rehearses.

Notwithstanding reasonable agribusiness and neighborhood food frameworks, the Supportable Food Development stresses the significance of decreasing food squander. Internationally, a lot of food is squandered at different phases of the inventory network, from creation and circulation to shopper families. This not just addresses a botched an open door to reduce hunger yet additionally adds to ozone harming substance discharges and other natural issues. By diminishing food squander, we can utilize the assets and energy put resources into food creation.

The development likewise requires a reexamination of our dietary decisions. An eating regimen that is focused on plant-based food sources, with a decreased accentuation on meat and dairy, is viewed as more manageable and empowering. Creature farming is a significant supporter of ozone harming substance outflows, deforestation, and water contamination. By embracing a more plant-based diet, people can fundamentally lessen their carbon impression and advance better wellbeing.

Besides, the Supportable Food Development advocates for straightforwardness and detectability in the food production network. Shoppers reserve the option to know where their food comes from, the way things were created, and under what conditions. Food naming and certificates, like natural, fair exchange, and non-GMO, assist shoppers with settling on informed decisions about the items they buy, lining up with their qualities and supportability objectives.

The development likewise brings up significant moral issues about the treatment of creatures in farming. Production line cultivating rehearses have gone under examination for their obtuse treatment of creatures, as well as their natural and wellbeing influences. The Reasonable Food Development advances animal government assistance by supporting practices, for example, confine free, free roaming, and field raised animal cultivating. This guarantees more altruistic treatment of creatures as well as has ecological advantages, like lessening the requirement for anti-toxins and moderating water contamination.

Maintainable food drives stretch out past the ranch and the kitchen. They additionally include the manner in which we convey and advertise food. Nearby ranchers' business sectors, local area upheld horticulture (CSA) projects, and food cooperatives are instances of elective food dispersion models that carry purchasers nearer to the wellspring of their food and backing neighborhood makers. These drives cultivate direct associations among shoppers and ranchers, advance a feeling of local area, and diminish the carbon impression related with food dispersion.

One more critical component of the Manageable Food Development is food sway. This idea attests that networks and countries ought to have command over their own food frameworks and assets. It challenges the strength of enormous partnerships in the worldwide food industry and calls for more just dynamic in food strategy. Food power perceives that the necessities and inclinations of nearby networks ought to direct food creation and circulation.

Food equity is intently attached to food power and addresses the imbalances present in the ongoing food framework. Many minimized networks need admittance to new, sound, and reasonable food, prompting diet-related wellbeing variations. Food equity advocates for evenhanded admittance to nutritious food and looks to dispense with food deserts — regions where occupants have restricted admittance to supermarkets or new produce. It likewise upholds drives that engage impeded networks to assume command over their food frameworks.

The Maintainable Food Development isn't restricted to one district or culture; it is a worldwide exertion. Various nations and networks have adjusted the standards of maintainability to their own special settings. For instance, in France, the "slow food" development, or "cooking du terroir," underlines the significance of nearby, conventional food and culinary practices. In Japan, the "mottainai" reasoning advances limiting waste and capitalizing on accessible assets.

The development has additionally gotten some decent forward movement in instructive establishments. Numerous colleges and schools have integrated manageability into their food administrations, offering privately obtained, natural, and morally created food to understudies. These establishments model supportable practices as well as teach the cutting edge about the significance of dependable food decisions.

At the public authority level, a few nations have perceived the meaning of the Reasonable Food Development and have done whatever it takes to advance maintainability in food frameworks. For example, the European Association has acquainted arrangements and guidelines with help maintainable horticulture, lessen food squander, and advance natural cultivating. Also, the US has different projects and drives pointed toward progressing maintainable food rehearses, for example, the Homestead to School program and backing for natural cultivating.

The Manageable Food Development likewise converges with ecological worries, as the food framework is firmly connected to environmental change. Agribusiness, transportation, and food squander are significant supporters of ozone depleting substance emanations. Supportable food rehearses, like natural cultivating and decreasing food miles, can assist with moderating these ecological effects. Also, regenerative horticulture rehearses, which center around building solid soil and sequestering carbon, certainly stand out for their capability to battle environmental change.

One more part of the development is the protection of biodiversity. Present day horticulture has frequently prompted the deficiency of different plant and animal species, as monocultures and modern cultivating rehearses overwhelm the scene. Supportable horticulture, with its accentuation on crop variety and biological system wellbeing, safeguards biodiversity by making natural surroundings for a large number of animal categories.

Water preservation is a major problem in economical food frameworks. Farming is a significant customer of water, and wasteful water system practices can drain nearby water assets. Maintainable horticulture advances water-saving strategies, for example, dribble water system and water gathering, as well as lessening the utilization of water-escalated crops in dry locales.

The Feasible Food Development isn't just about ecological supportability yet additionally about friendly and financial maintainability. It recognizes the difficulties looked by limited scope ranchers and tries to enable them through fair exchange practices and backing for their neighborhood economies. At times, this development has assisted networks with recapturing command over their food frameworks and become less subject to worldwide organizations.

Food security is a basic issue that the Maintainable Food Development addresses. By advancing manageable and neighborhood food frameworks, the development can upgrade food security by lessening dependence on worldwide inventory anchors that are powerless against interruptions. The Coronavirus pandemic featured the weaknesses of such stock chains, presenting a defense for reinforcing nearby and provincial food frameworks.

The development has likewise caused to notice the issue of food power even with economic deals that might restrict a country's capacity to direct its own food framework. Some contend that global economic alliance can sabotage food sway by focusing on corporate interests over nearby direction.

Purchaser mindfulness and support assume a fundamental part in the Reasonable Food Development. As people become more educated about the natural and moral ramifications of their food decisions, they are bound to help feasible practices and request change from food makers and policymakers. Online entertainment and computerized stages have been instrumental in bringing issues to light and assembling buyers to help economical food drives.

2.1 The rise of sustainability in food production

The cutting edge food creation framework is going through a significant change, driven by a developing acknowledgment of the dire need to address the natural, social, and wellbeing influences related with the manner in which we produce, circulate, and eat food. This shift toward maintainability in food creation is a reaction to the interconnected worldwide difficulties of environmental change, asset consumption, food uncertainty, and social disparity. This article investigates the diverse ascent of supportability in food creation, following its development, key drivers, and the different manners by which it is appearing across the globe.

Maintainability in food creation envelops a scope of practices, standards, and objectives pointed toward accomplishing a more amicable and adjusted connection between human action and the regular world. It is driven by the figuring out that our ongoing food framework, portrayed by modern farming, significant distance food transportation, and inefficient utilization designs, is neither biologically economical nor socially. The ascent of maintainability in food creation mirrors a more extensive change in cultural qualities and needs, with a rising accentuation on natural stewardship, social value, and general wellbeing.

One of the basic parts of the manageability development in food creation is the progress from regular, compound serious agribusiness to additional feasible cultivating rehearses. Customary horticulture, which depends vigorously on manufactured pesticides, herbicides, and manures, has been related with negative natural effects, including soil debasement, water contamination, and the deficiency of biodiversity. Conversely, feasible cultivating rehearses focus on natural strategies, crop revolution, and the utilization of normal composts and vermin control measures. This shift expects to keep up with the strength of soils, lessen compound information sources, and limit the biological impression of agribusiness.

Nearby and limited scope cultivating is one more foundation of economical food creation. The accentuation on nearby food frameworks is established in limiting the carbon impression related with food creation and appropriation. By diminishing transportation distances and cultivating provincial food organizations, neighborhood cultivating rehearses decline ozone depleting substance emanations as well as help local area versatility and monetary turn of events. Limited scope ranchers are frequently at the front of feasible food creation, embracing natural cultivating strategies, moral treatment of animals, and fair work rehearses.

The decrease of food squander is a necessary part of the manageability development. Across the globe, a disturbing measure of food is squandered at different phases of the store network, from creation and conveyance to customer families. This not just addresses a botched an open door to ease hunger yet additionally adds to ozone depleting substance outflows and other ecological issues. Tending to food squander is a basic move toward utilizing the assets and energy put resources into food creation, decreasing the stress on the climate.

Moreover, the maintainability development puts a huge spotlight on rethinking dietary decisions. An eating regimen that focuses on plant-based food varieties, with a decreased accentuation on meat and dairy, is viewed as more feasible and fortifying. The creation of creature based food varieties is a significant supporter of ozone harming substance discharges, deforestation, and water contamination. By taking on a more plant-based diet, people can fundamentally diminish their carbon impression and advance better wellbeing results.

The maintainability development likewise calls for straightforwardness and discernibility in the food store network. Customers reserve the privilege to know where their food comes from, the way things were created, and under what conditions. Food marking and certificates, like natural, fair exchange, and non-GMO, assist buyers with pursuing informed decisions about the items they buy, lining up with their qualities and maintainability objectives. This straightforwardness enables buyers to help practices and items that are more in accordance with their moral and natural worries.

Moral contemplations reach out to the treatment of creatures in farming, another basic issue that the manageability development addresses. Production line cultivating rehearses have gone under investigation for their heartless treatment of creatures, as well as their ecological and wellbeing influences.

Reasonable food creation advocates for animal government assistance by supporting practices, for example, confine free, unfenced, and field raised animal cultivating. This guarantees more empathetic treatment of creatures as well as has ecological advantages, like decreasing the requirement for anti-infection agents and moderating water contamination.

Reasonable food drives envelop the homestead and the kitchen as well as how food is circulated and advertised. Nearby ranchers' business sectors, local area upheld farming (CSA) projects, and food cooperatives are instances of elective food circulation models that carry customers nearer to the wellspring of their food and backing neighborhood makers. These drives cultivate direct associations among purchasers and ranchers, advance a feeling of local area, and diminish the carbon impression related with food dispersion.

One more huge component of the maintainability development is the idea of food sway. Food sway declares that networks and countries ought to have command over their own food frameworks and assets. It challenges the strength of enormous organizations in the worldwide food industry and calls for more fair dynamic in food strategy. Food power perceives that the requirements and inclinations of nearby networks ought to direct food creation and dissemination.

Food equity is firmly connected to food sway and addresses the imbalances present in the ongoing food framework. Many underestimated networks need admittance to new, sound, and reasonable food, prompting diet-related wellbeing variations. Food equity advocates for fair admittance to nutritious food and looks to dispense with food deserts — regions where occupants have restricted admittance to supermarkets or new produce. It additionally upholds drives that engage burdened networks to assume command over their food frameworks.

The maintainability development isn't restricted to a specific locale or culture; a worldwide exertion takes on various structures in different settings. Various nations and networks have adjusted the standards of manageability to their exceptional conditions. For instance, in France, the "slow food" development, or "cooking du terroir," underscores the significance of neighborhood, conventional food and culinary practices. In Japan, the "mottainai" reasoning advances limiting waste and taking full advantage of accessible assets.

The development has likewise made advances in instructive establishments. Numerous colleges and schools have integrated maintainability into their food administrations, offering privately obtained, natural, and morally delivered food to understudies. These establishments model supportable practices as well as instruct the cutting edge about the significance of dependable food decisions.

At the public authority level, a few nations have perceived the meaning of the supportability development and have done whatever it takes to advance manageability in food frameworks.

For example, the European Association has acquainted arrangements and guidelines with help supportable horticulture, lessen food squander, and advance natural cultivating. Additionally, the US has different projects and drives pointed toward progressing maintainable food rehearses, for example, the Ranch to School program and backing for natural cultivating.

The manageability development additionally crosses with ecological worries, as the food framework is firmly connected to environmental change. Farming, transportation, and food squander are significant supporters of ozone depleting substance discharges. Supportable food rehearses, like natural cultivating and diminishing food miles, can assist with relieving these ecological effects. Also, regenerative horticulture rehearses, which center around building sound soil and sequestering carbon, certainly stand out for their capability to battle environmental change.

Biodiversity preservation is one more significant component of the manageability development. Current horticulture has frequently prompted the deficiency of different plant and animal species, as monocultures and modern cultivating rehearses overwhelm the scene. Economical farming, with its accentuation on crop variety and biological system wellbeing, safeguards biodiversity by making natural surroundings for a great many animal groups.

Water protection is a major problem in maintainable food frameworks. Horticulture is a significant purchaser of water, and wasteful water system practices can drain neighborhood water assets. Manageable horticulture advances water-saving methods, for example, trickle water system and water gathering, as well as lessening the utilization of water-serious harvests in dry areas.

The maintainability development isn't just about natural manageability yet additionally about friendly and monetary supportability. It recognizes the difficulties looked by limited scope ranchers and looks to engage them through fair exchange practices and backing for their nearby economies. At times, this development has assisted networks with recapturing command over their food frameworks and become less subject to global partnerships.

Food security is a basic issue that the manageability development addresses. By advancing practical and neighborhood food frameworks, the development can improve food security by decreasing dependence on worldwide stock anchors that are powerless against disturbances. The Coronavirus pandemic featured the weaknesses of such inventory chains, presenting a defense for reinforcing neighborhood and provincial food frameworks.

The development has likewise caused to notice the issue of food sway notwithstanding economic deals that might restrict a country's capacity to control its own food framework. Some contend that international.

2.2 Benefits of sustainable farming

Reasonable cultivating, frequently alluded to as regenerative or eco-accommodating farming, is picking up speeding up as a reaction to the various natural, monetary, and social difficulties confronting our reality. This technique for food creation tries to limit damage to the climate, advance biodiversity, and backing country networks while giving nutritious food to a developing worldwide populace. In this paper, we will investigate the broad cluster of advantages related with practical cultivating, going from natural benefits to monetary and social advantages.

One of the most apparent and major benefits of reasonable cultivating is its commitment to natural conservation and rebuilding. Conventional, modern cultivating rehearses unfavorably affect the climate, like soil corruption, water contamination, and deforestation. Manageable cultivating, then again, looks to limit these adverse consequences and may try and attempt to reestablish biological systems.

Soil preservation and improvement are essential focal points of economical cultivating. Through rehearses like harvest pivot, cover editing, and negligible culturing, supportable ranchers assemble and keep up with solid soils. These practices assist with forestalling soil disintegration and corruption, upgrade soil ripeness, and advance carbon sequestration, which can moderate environmental change by eliminating carbon dioxide from the climate.

Furthermore, practical cultivating underscores the decrease of substance inputs, like engineered pesticides and composts. This limits the defilement of soil and water with unsafe synthetic compounds, which can adversely affect environments and human wellbeing. By decreasing synthetic use, reasonable cultivating safeguards pollinators, amphibian life, and other basic parts of normal biological systems.

Biodiversity protection is one more imperative part of reasonable cultivating. Modern farming has frequently prompted the making of monocultures, where huge areas of land are committed to a solitary yield. This training can have unfortunate results, like decreased biodiversity and an expanded weakness to irritations and sicknesses. Feasible cultivating, conversely, energizes crop variety, which gives natural surroundings and food to a great many animal groups. By keeping up with assorted environments close by their homesteads, practical ranchers add to the conservation of natural life and local plant species.

Water protection and quality improvement are additionally key advantages of practical cultivating. Productive water system strategies, for example, trickle water system and water collecting, assist with limiting water use, which is basic in districts confronting water shortage. Also, reasonable cultivating rehearses lessen the spillover of supplements and synthetics into water bodies, moderating water contamination and defending amphibian environments.

One of the most squeezing worldwide difficulties is environmental change, which is firmly connected to farming and land use. Reasonable cultivating, with its emphasis on carbon sequestration, is viewed as a likely answer for address this test.

By further developing soil wellbeing and expanding natural matter substance, reasonable cultivating practices can catch and store carbon dioxide in the dirt. This mitigates environmental change as well as improves the flexibility of homesteads to outrageous climate occasions.

Monetary advantages are one more huge part of reasonable cultivating. While there might be starting expenses related with progressing to supportable practices, the drawn out financial benefits are significant. Economical cultivating strategies can decrease the requirement for expensive sources of info like engineered pesticides and manures. Also, by upgrading soil wellbeing, supportable cultivating can build yields and harvest quality, prompting worked on financial returns for ranchers.

Reasonable cultivating can likewise set out financial open doors in provincial regions. The accentuation on nearby and limited scope agribusiness can reinforce neighborhood economies by supporting little ranchers and animating local area improvement. The utilization of privately adjusted and various harvests can give different attractive items, further expanding nearby economies. Furthermore, by lessening the requirement for significant distance transportation of food, reasonable cultivating can bring down transportation expenses and energy utilization, adding to a more proficient and practical food framework.

Rural flexibility is a vital monetary advantage of maintainable cultivating. Maintainable practices assist ranches with adjusting to changing ecological circumstances, whether it be moving environment designs, arising irritations, or fluctuating business sectors. By differentiating harvests and utilizing natural strategies for bother the executives, feasible ranches are many times more ready to weather conditions difficulties and vulnerabilities in the horticultural area.

Reasonable cultivating is additionally connected with further developed food quality and security. The decrease of substance inputs and the accentuation on soil wellbeing frequently bring about better, more nutritious yields. Likewise, reasonable cultivating rehearses, like natural techniques, advance the aversion of destructive synthetic compounds, which can affect the two shoppers and farmworkers.

Also, manageable cultivating focuses on moral and compassionate treatment of creatures. Dissimilar to industrial facility cultivating, which is frequently connected with packed and harsh circumstances, maintainable cultivating rehearses support animal government assistance by giving more space, admittance to the outside, and better everyday environments for livestock. This lines up with moral worries as well as makes positive natural impacts, like diminished utilization of anti-infection agents and the relief of water contamination.

Customer interest for reasonable items is on the ascent. As individuals become more mindful of the natural and moral ramifications of their food decisions, they search out reasonably created food sources. This developing interest presents financial open doors for ranchers who embrace supportable practices.

Reasonable cultivating can draw in an exceptional cost, mirroring the additional worth of earth and morally mindful food creation. Ranchers who line up with shopper inclinations for supportability might end up in a more grounded market position.

Notwithstanding the ecological and monetary benefits of supportable cultivating, there are various social advantages related with this way to deal with horticulture. Feasible cultivating rehearses frequently focus on local area and social prosperity, perceiving that a solid and energetic rustic local area is fundamental for the progress of maintainable horticulture.

One of the focal standards of reasonable cultivating is the help of nearby and limited scope horticulture. This approach fortifies nearby networks by setting out monetary open doors, cultivating connections among ranchers and purchasers, and safeguarding the rustic lifestyle. By obtaining food locally, shoppers can feel more associated with their food and individuals who produce it, which can have social and social importance.

Neighborhood ranchers' business sectors, local area upheld agribusiness (CSA) projects, and food cooperatives are instances of drives that carry shoppers nearer to the wellspring of their food and backing nearby makers. These elective food dissemination models encourage direct associations among purchasers and ranchers, advance a feeling of local area, and lessen the carbon impression related with food conveyance. They likewise add to food security by upgrading admittance to new, privately delivered food.

Food equity is one more friendly part of supportable cultivating. Many under-estimated networks need admittance to new, solid, and reasonable food, prompting diet-related wellbeing variations. Maintainable cultivating practices can resolve these issues by giving impartial admittance to nutritious food and dispensing with food deserts — regions where inhabitants have restricted admittance to supermarkets or new produce. This civil rights part of economical cultivating lines up with the more extensive objective of guaranteeing that all people have the potential chance to pursue quality food decisions.

The reasonable cultivating development upholds food power, an idea that declares networks and countries ought to have command over their own food frameworks and assets. Food power difficulties the strength of huge partnerships in the worldwide food industry and calls for more equitable dynamic in food strategy. It perceives that neighborhood networks ought to be engaged to shape their own food creation and conveyance frameworks as per their requirements and values.

The ascent of maintainability in food creation isn't restricted to one district or culture; it is a worldwide exertion. Various nations and networks have adjusted the standards of manageability to their own remarkable settings and difficulties. The development has taken on different structures, mirroring the variety of agrarian practices, biological systems, and social qualities all over the planet.

For instance, in France, the "slow food" development, or "cooking du terroir," accentuates the significance of nearby, customary food and culinary practices. It praises the social meaning of food and energizes the conservation of neighborhood food customs. In Japan, the "mottainai" reasoning advances limiting waste and taking advantage of accessible assets. This idea lines up with manageability by empowering frugality and a decrease of waste.

At the public authority level, a few nations have perceived the meaning of the supportability development and have done whatever it may take to advance maintainability in food frameworks. The European Association, for instance, has acquainted approaches and guidelines with help supportable agribusiness, lessen food squander, and advance natural cultivating. Essentially, the US has different projects and drives pointed toward progressing feasible food rehearses, for example, the Homestead to School program and backing for natural cultivating.

2.3 Challenges and barriers

While economical cultivating offers various advantages, it likewise faces different difficulties and hindrances that block its boundless reception and achievement. These impediments range from monetary limitations to social and political elements. In this exposition, we will investigate the critical difficulties and obstructions that practical cultivating experiences, as well as likely methodologies to defeat them.

Financial Difficulties: One of the premier difficulties in supportable cultivating is the monetary hindrance. Changing from regular, modern farming to supportable strategies can be expensive and may require interests in new gear, preparing, and foundation. The underlying capital expected to roll out these improvements can be a huge hindrance for some ranchers, especially limited scope and asset compelled makers. The apparent monetary dangers related with changing to maintainable practices can deter a few ranchers from making the primary strides.

Arrangement: Government impetuses, awards, and appropriations can assist with moderating financial hindrances. Monetary help for manageable cultivating practices can make it more open for little and medium-sized ranches. Likewise, helpful models, where ranchers pool assets and information, can diminish individual expenses and advance maintainability.

Restricted Information and Schooling: Numerous ranchers come up short on information and preparing important to actually carry out manageable practices. Maintainable cultivating frequently requires an alternate arrangement of abilities and methods contrasted with ordinary cultivating. Ranchers might be new to edit revolution, natural vermin control, or regenerative soil the board. An absence of training and mindfulness about manageable cultivating techniques can be a critical hindrance.

Arrangement: Giving preparation and instructive assets to ranchers is fundamental. Government and non-benefit associations can offer studios, courses, and expansion administrations to assist ranchers with learning reasonable methods. Dividing examples of overcoming adversity and best practices between the cultivating local area can likewise assist with connecting the information hole.

Protection from Change: Protection from change is a typical boundary to the reception of economical cultivating rehearses. A few ranchers might be reluctant to change from natural techniques and innovations. There might be worries about diminished yields during the change time frame or vulnerabilities about the monetary reasonability of economical cultivating.

Arrangement: Showing the drawn out advantages of maintainability, including expanded soil ripeness, decreased input costs, and further developed crop strength, can assist with lightening obstruction. Giving contextual analyses and displaying fruitful changes can rouse trust in the viability of manageable cultivating.

Market Access and Circulation: Feasible ranchers frequently face difficulties in getting to business sectors and conveying their items. While buyer interest for reasonable items is developing, ordinary inventory chains and conveyance organizations can make it challenging for manageable items to arrive at purchasers. Feasible ranches might be geologically secluded, making it trying to associate with metropolitan or far off business sectors.

Arrangement: Supporting nearby and territorial food frameworks can assist with crossing over the market access hole. Ranchers' business sectors, local area upheld horticulture (CSA) programs, and direct-to-buyer deals can furnish maintainable ranchers with closer associations with purchasers. In addition, policymakers can boost the improvement of elective appropriation networks that help practical items.

Increasing: Increasing reasonable cultivating practices to fulfill the worldwide need for food while keeping up with maintainability is a perplexing test. Numerous manageable practices are work serious and may not be quickly adaptable without undermining their natural and social advantages.

Arrangement: Empowering territorial and public strategies that advance manageable horticulture can work with the increasing of these practices. Supporting feasible cultivating cooperatives and associations can likewise assist with pooling assets and information, making it more straightforward to embrace these practices for a bigger scope.

Land and Asset Accessibility: Maintainable cultivating frequently requires more land and assets than customary practices, particularly while expanding yields and involving land for environmental rebuilding. The accessibility of reasonable land and assets can be a restricting component in certain districts.

Arrangement: Land-use approaches that safeguard farmland and focus on maintainable agribusiness can be advantageous. Government drives that energize land preservation and feasible land the executives can assist with protecting regular assets for economical cultivating. In locales with restricted land accessibility, metropolitan and peri-metropolitan cultivating can be
an answer.

Administrative Obstructions: Administrative systems may not necessarily support feasible cultivating rehearses. Now and again, guidelines might lean toward traditional horticulture or prevent manageable other options. For example, natural certificate cycles can be difficult for limited scope ranchers.

Arrangement: Support endeavors and strategy changes can assist with establishing a better administrative climate for feasible cultivating. Smoothing out affirmation processes, making monetary motivators, and giving legitimate securities to supportable practices can eliminate administrative hindrances.

Social and Cultural Obstructions: Social perspectives and cultural insights can be boundaries to reasonable cultivating. A few networks and people might be impervious to changing conventional cultivating rehearses. Furthermore, there can be an absence of appreciation for the ecological and social advantages of economical cultivating in the public eye at large.

Arrangement: Bringing issues to light and instructing the general population about the advantages of supportable cultivating can assist with moving social mentalities. Public missions, local area commitment, and instructive drives can challenge assumptions about cultivating and advance a more supportable ethos.

Land Residency and Possession: Land residency and proprietorship issues can block the reception of supportable cultivating. At times, land might be possessed by truant property managers or corporate elements that focus on benefit over supportability. This can restrict ranchers' capacity to make long haul interests in maintainable practices.

Arrangement: Tending to land residency issues through land change or approaches that favor feasible land the executives can assist with beating this obstruction. Supporting drives that empower land access for reasonable cultivating, for example, land trusts or local area land cooperatives, can give secure land residency to manageable ranchers.

Market Rivalry: Maintainable ranchers might confront contest from bigger, modern scale cultivates that can create at lower costs because of economies of scale. This opposition can come down on practical ranchers, making it trying for them to contend in the commercial center.

Arrangement: Making market components that esteem supportability and give a premium to feasible items can assist with evening the odds. Shopper training about the genuine expenses of regular horticulture, including ecological and social effects, can energize support for manageable items, even at a greater cost point.

Admittance to Credit and Funding: Admittance to credit and supporting is vital for ranchers hoping to put resources into reasonable practices. Notwithstanding, some limited scale ranchers, particularly in non-industrial nations, face hardships in getting to reasonable credit and funding choices.

Arrangement: Government and non-administrative associations can give miniature advances and credit programs custom fitted to the requirements of practical ranchers. These projects can uphold interests in maintainable practices and lessen monetary boundaries.

Environmental Change and Outrageous Climate Occasions: Environmental change presents huge difficulties to cultivating as a general rule, and reasonable cultivating is no special case. Progressively eccentric weather conditions, dry spells, floods, and outrageous occasions can disturb cultivating tasks and block the capacity to plan and carry out manageable practices.

Arrangement: Manageable cultivating rehearses, for example, cover trimming and agroforestry, can improve the versatility of homesteads to environmental change. Examination and advancement in maintainable cultivating can assist with growing new procedures for adjusting to an evolving environment.

Institutional Help and Exploration: The absence of institutional help and examination financing for manageable cultivating is a huge boundary. Customary farming has generally gotten more examination financing and government support, prompting an abundance of information and innovation in this area.

Arrangement: Moving examination needs and expanding subsidizing for reasonable cultivating can offer the vital help for advancement and the improvement of manageable practices. Government interest in horticultural innovative work can be diverted to focus on maintainability.

Inventory network Intricacy: Incorporating reasonable cultivating into complex stockpile chains can challenge. Planning the obtaining, certificate, and conveyance of reasonable items requires participation and strategic exertion.

Arrangement: Creating straightforward and detectable stockpile chains can improve on this intricacy. The utilization of blockchain innovation, advanced stages, and accreditation frameworks can improve store network straightforwardness, making it simpler for customers to get to manageable items.

Shopper Inclinations and Mindfulness: While buyer interest for supportable items is developing, it isn't uniform across all districts and socioeconomics. A few customers might focus on low costs over manageability, and others might need mindfulness about the ecological and moral ramifications of their food decisions.

Arrangement: Shopper training and mindfulness missions can assist with overcoming any issues in buyer inclinations. Featuring the advantages of maintainable cultivating and its positive effect on the climate, nearby networks, and wellbeing can urge more shoppers to pick reasonable production.

Chapter 3

Locally Sourced and Fresh

In a world that has been persistently reshaped by the fast development of innovation, the idea of "privately obtained and new" has taken on new importance. As we look forward to the year 2100, obviously our relationship with food and our current circumstance has gone through a significant change.

The 21st century was a critical period in mankind's set of experiences, set apart by an uncommon speed increase of urbanization, populace development, and mechanical progression. In the early many years of the 100 years, the worldwide food framework confronted tremendous difficulties, including overpopulation, asset exhaustion, and environmental change. These moves constrained us to reexamine our way to deal with food creation and dispersion.

Quite possibly of the main change in our relationship with food was the reappearance of neighborhood and new as core values for our food frameworks. The requests of a developing populace, combined with an extending consciousness of the natural results of globalized food creation and dissemination, provoked a renaissance in neighborhood horticulture and the prioritization of new, occasional fixings.

The time of rambling modern horticulture, set apart by monoculture cultivating, weighty pesticide use, and significant distance transportation, had started to show its inadequacies. Soil debasement, water contamination, and the deficiency of biodiversity were only a couple of the adverse consequences. Accordingly, people group and state run administrations all over the planet began to put resources into more manageable and privately engaged food frameworks.

As we excursion to 2100, the tradition of these progressions is evident in the manner we produce, circulate, and eat food. The shift to privately obtained and new food has rejuvenated nearby economies as well as significantly affected our wellbeing, the climate, and the manner in which we associate with our food.

The reception of nearby food frameworks has rejuvenated country regions, encouraging financial development and giving new open doors to ranchers. During the 21st hundred years, as worries about food security developed, states and networks put resources into supporting neighborhood agribusiness. They executed approaches and motivations that empowered limited scope cultivating, enhanced crop creation, and the conservation of legacy assortments.

Subsequently, little ranches and nearby food makers started to flourish. Ranchers' business sectors, local area upheld horticulture (CSA) programs, and metropolitan nurseries became vital pieces of our food scene. Purchasers began to rediscover the delight of knowing their ranchers and food makers specifically, encouraging a feeling of trust and association that was missing in the time of unknown, efficiently manufactured food.

The idea of "ranch to-table" developed from a popular café trademark to a basic standard of food obtaining. Cafés and families the same started focusing on the utilization of neighborhood, occasional fixings. The center moved from frozen and handled food varieties to new, privately developed produce. This shift improved the kinds of our dinners as well as significantly affected our wellbeing.

With the resurgence of nearby horticulture, there was a restored accentuation on the dietary benefit of new, natural food sources. Individuals began to consume a more extensive assortment of leafy foods, as occasional accessibility directed their weight control plans. The diminished dependence on handled food varieties prompted a huge decrease in diet-related medical problems, like heftiness and coronary illness.

This dietary change had flowing impacts on medical care frameworks, with lower interest for meds and therapies connected with diet-incited ailments. Individuals started to comprehend that food could be both medication and food. The possibility of food as an all encompassing way to deal with prosperity got momentum, and the world saw a critical diminishing in way of life related medical issues.

Notwithstanding the significant effect on our wellbeing, the renaissance of privately obtained and new food assumed a critical part in the more extensive work to address environmental change. In the mid 21st 100 years, worries about the carbon impression of food creation and transportation prompted a reexamination of our globalized food frameworks. The broad transportation of food from far off districts was perceived as a significant supporter of ozone harming substance outflows.

Limiting food creation was a reaction to these natural worries as well as a proactive way to deal with moderating the impacts of environmental change. As fossil fuel by-products turned out to be progressively managed, the ecological effect of significant distance food transportation was examined, prompting tremendous changes in our food production network.

The decrease in significant distance food transportation decidedly affected fossil fuel byproducts, as well as on air quality and gridlock in metropolitan regions. The subsequent decline in food miles not just diminished the carbon impression of our dinners yet in addition added to cleaner and more economical urban areas.

Neighborhood horticulture additionally introduced a chance to carry out creative, harmless to the ecosystem cultivating rehearses. Feasible cultivating techniques, for example, permaculture, agroforestry, and regenerative agribusiness, acquired noticeable quality. These practices improved the dirt and expanded biodiversity as well as added to carbon sequestration, assisting with combatting environmental change.

The accentuation on nearby food frameworks prompted a resurgence of legacy and legacy crops, which had been minimized in the time of modern farming. Ranchers, upheld by nearby networks and buyers, started to focus on the conservation of these interesting and various yield assortments. This shift significantly affected biodiversity and food security.

The development and utilization of legacy and legacy crops assisted protect the hereditary variety of our food with providing. In a world progressively defenseless against the impacts of environmental change and pandemics, these one of a kind harvest assortments gave versatility. They were many times better adjusted to neighborhood conditions and more impervious to vermin and sicknesses.

The expanded accentuation on biodiversity affected our environments. As different harvests were once again introduced, so were different environments. Ranchers incorporated different plant species and even animals into their farming scenes, establishing a more amicable and strong climate.

The advancement of biodiversity stretched out to the set of all animals also. Limited scope, nearby animals cultivating turned into a favored strategy for meat creation. Buyers were able to pay something else for meat that was raised morally and economically, and the center moved from processing plant ranches to fed and grass-took care of animals.

Because of worries about creature government assistance and natural effect, states and networks forced stricter guidelines on the meat and dairy industry. These guidelines intended to decrease the negative natural results of enormous scope domesticated animals creation and to guarantee the sympathetic treatment of creatures.

Subsequently, the meat business went through huge changes. Processing plant ranches, portrayed by stuffed and coldhearted circumstances, dwindled in number. The pattern of bringing creatures up in additional compassionate and normal circumstances significantly affected the nature of meat and dairy items. Buyers were able to pay something else for these items, grasping the significance of supporting moral and economical cultivating rehearses.

The shift towards privately obtained and new food was not restricted to the US or Europe. It turned into a worldwide peculiarity, with each locale of the world embracing these standards in extraordinary ways. In Asia, for instance, customary cultivating rehearses like rice paddies and terraced horticulture encountered a restoration. The fastidious consideration taken in developing rice and other staple yields, joined with the utilization of neighborhood and occasional fixings, made another appreciation for Asian cooking.

In Africa, nearby food frameworks developed to address explicit difficulties. Dry season safe yields, similar to millet and sorghum, acquired noticeable quality in dry districts, giving a more maintainable food source. Local area based agribusiness and cooperatives engaged neighborhood ranchers to take care of their networks while protecting normal assets.

In South America, the Amazon rainforest, when under the danger of deforestation, turned into a point of convergence for economical and native horticulture. Nearby people group tracked down inventive ways of developing harvests and keep up with the rich biodiversity of the rainforest while additionally creating new and nutritious nourishment for their own utilization and worldwide business sectors.

The Center East embraced its rich culinary customs, rethinking its old food culture with a cutting edge turn. Nearby business sectors, known as souks, kept on being lively centers of action, exhibiting the freshest fixings and safeguarding culinary legacy.

In the polar locales, where the impacts of environmental change were most articulated, creative ways to deal with food creation arose. Nurseries and hydroponics frameworks took into consideration the all year development of new produce. Neighborhood people group adjusted to new food frameworks, utilizing environmentally friendly power sources and economical fishing practices to guarantee food security.

With this multitude of changes, the world saw a resurgence in social variety and a more profound appreciation for neighborhood culinary customs. Individuals commended the flavors, surfaces, and stories behind their food. The rich embroidered artwork of worldwide cooking was woven with strings of supportability and local area strength.

As the year 2100 unfurled, innovation kept on assuming a huge part in molding the manner in which we collaborated with privately obtained and new food. The computerized age, which had its beginnings in the twentieth hundred years, had developed, offering a heap of instruments and stages that upset the manner in which we developed, bought, and arranged our food.

Savvy agribusiness had turned into the standard, with ranches furnished with sensors, drones, and computerized reasoning. These advancements assisted ranchers with improving harvest the executives, screen ecological circumstances, and lessen asset squander. Accuracy farming considered more productive utilization of water, manures, and pesticides, bringing about better yields and a decreased ecological effect.

The Web of Things (IoT) assumed a crucial part in interfacing nearby ranchers and shoppers. Brilliant fridges and storerooms followed food stock and newness, decreasing food squander. Purchasers got continuous data on the accessibility of neighborhood produce and the best recipes for their fixings. Food squander was definitely decreased, and individuals turned out to be more aware of their utilization designs.

Blockchain innovation, initially intended for secure and straightforward monetary exchanges, was adjusted to make discernible food supply chains. Purchasers could undoubtedly get to data about the beginning of their food, from the homestead to the table. Food handling and detectability became central, as shoppers requested responsibility following various food-related wellbeing alarms.

Man-made brainpower (artificial intelligence) reformed food creation, appropriation, and planning. Calculations broke down weather conditions, market interest, and neighborhood crop yields, empowering ranchers to settle on information driven choices. Computer based intelligence fueled robots helped with planting, gathering, and bundling crops, lessening the requirement for difficult work and expanding proficiency.

In the kitchen, artificial intelligence driven recipe generators considered individual dietary inclinations and healthful necessities, offering customized dinner plans. Shrewd broilers and preparing machines guaranteed that feasts were ready flawlessly, decreasing the requirement for culinary mastery and limiting food squander.

3D printing innovation developed to make altered food things, empowering people to plan their own dinners in view of their nourishing prerequisites and taste inclinations. The time of efficiently manufactured, one-size-fits-all food had given way to another period of personalization.

The food conveyance scene additionally went through critical changes. Independent vehicles and robots, directed by artificial intelligence, guaranteed quick and proficient conveyance of new, privately obtained feasts. These conveyance frameworks decreased gridlock as well as brought down the carbon impression of the food store network.

The ascent of the gig economy prompted a multiplication of food conveyance stages, where neighborhood prepares and food craftsmans could offer their manifestations straightforwardly to buyers. This direct-to-shopper model empowered neighborhood food makers to contact a more extensive crowd, encouraging monetary development in nearby networks.

The computerized age carried straightforwardness to the front of our food frameworks. Shoppers could follow the excursion of their food from field to fork, knowing precisely where their produce was developed and who played a part in its creation. This straightforwardness engaged shoppers to go with informed decisions about the food they bought and ate.

Sanitation was upgraded by blockchain innovation, empowering speedy distinguishing proof of the wellspring of any tainting. This killed the requirement for huge scope food reviews, as just impacted groups of items could be followed and taken out from the market. The confidence in the food production network was reinforced, and foodborne sicknesses became uncommon.

The worldwide food industry had likewise gone through a seismic change in its way to deal with squander. In the mid 21st hundred years, food squander was a gigantic issue, with tremendous measures of food disposed of at each phase of the production network. Be that as it may, by 2100, the world had gained huge headway in lessening and reusing food squander.

The ascent of roundabout food frameworks had turned into the standard. Squander from food creation and utilization was changed into important assets. Natural waste was treated the soil and got back to the dirt, advancing the nature of agrarian land.

Imaginative advancements had arisen to change over food squander into biofuels, decreasing our reliance on petroleum products and further moderating the impacts of environmental change.

The idea of "revolting" or "defective" produce had acquired broad acknowledgment. Buyers comprehended that leafy foods with minor restorative blemishes were similarly essentially as nutritious and delightful as their outwardly wonderful partners. This change in discernment significantly affected food squander, as a greater amount of these "terrible" produce things were remembered for the food supply.

The advanced age likewise worked with the production of online food-sharing stages, where people and networks could trade overflow food. These stages diminished food squander by reallocating overabundance food to those out of luck. It turned into a typical practice for families, cafés, and supermarkets to impart surplus food to neighborhood noble cause and food banks.

While the change of our food frameworks was driven by a bunch of mechanical advances, it was at last moored in a significant change in cultural qualities. Individuals in the year 2100 focused on manageability, wellbeing, and local area over accommodation and cost. They perceived that their decisions in their regular routines straightforwardly affected the soundness of the planet and the prosperity of people in the future.

This change in values reached out past food. It saturated each part of life, from transportation to energy utilization. As people group and people embraced a more reasonable lifestyle, they looked to live as one with the climate as opposed to taking advantage of it. The possibility of "supportability" was a popular expression as well as a major core value.

The advancement of the 21st century had not come without its difficulties, but rather the aggregate endeavors of people, networks, states, and organizations had made an existence where privately obtained and new food was not an extravagance but rather a major right. The new food frameworks were more fair, guaranteeing that all citizenry approached new, nutritious dinners.

The reappearance of nearby food frameworks had renewed provincial regions and more modest networks, prompting a more fair dissemination of riches and potential open doors. Ranchers, food craftsmans, and nearby food makers were praised for their commitments to society, and their occupations were safeguarded through approaches that guaranteed fair wages and admittance to medical care and schooling.

The worldwide local area perceived the significance of tending to food uncertainty, a major problem that had tormented the 21st hundred years. Aggregate endeavors to battle yearning and lack of healthy sustenance brought about food banks, local area nurseries, and drives to give nutritious dinners to underserved populaces. The right to food was revered in peaceful accords and turned into a foundation of the battle against destitution and disparity.

The excursion to 2100 was set apart by snapshots of motivation, strength, and advancement. The difficulties of the 21st century had been met sincerely and a significant change in values. The renaissance of privately obtained and new food was meaningful of a world that had come to focus on maintainability, wellbeing, and local area.

In the year 2100, as we thought back on the changes of our food frameworks, we saw an existence where our decisions as people and as a general public decidedly affected the planet. We comprehended that the food on our plates was food as well as an impression of our qualities and our obligation to a superior, more maintainable future.

3.1 Importance of local food sourcing

The significance of nearby food obtaining has filled dramatically in late many years, and as we dive into the subject, it turns out to be progressively evident that this isn't just a pattern yet a major change by they way we approach food creation and utilization. In the 21st hundred years, the globalized food framework confronted various difficulties, for example, ecological corruption, food handling concerns, and moral issues connected with creation rehearses. Accordingly, the idea of neighborhood food obtaining arose as an answer that tended to these squeezing worries while likewise conveying a large group of different advantages.

The worldwide food arrangement of the twentieth century was portrayed by an unpredictable snare of creation, dissemination, and utilization that spread over landmasses. Large scale manufacturing, significant distance transportation, and brought together dissemination networks were the standard, promising accommodation and reasonableness.

In any case, this framework came at an extensive expense. As food made a trip immense distances to arrive at buyers, it ate huge measures of energy and assets, adding to ecological debasement and environmental change.

One of the most squeezing concerns was the carbon impression of our food. The transportation of merchandise across landmasses produced significant ozone harming substance discharges. Devouring food that had voyaged large number of miles turned out to be progressively unreasonable notwithstanding mounting proof of the results of environmental change. The ecological effect of our food decisions was difficult to disregard.

Moreover, the globalized food framework prompted a separation among buyers and the wellsprings of their food. Individuals frequently had little information on where their food came from, who delivered it, or the circumstances under which it was developed. The absence of straightforwardness and responsibility in the food store network raised worries about sanitation, moral creation rehearses, and the treatment of horticultural workers.

The ascent of modern agribusiness, set apart by monoculture cultivating, weighty pesticide use, and the consumption of regular assets, was another major problem. As farming practices zeroed in on productivity and scale, they frequently came to the detriment of soil wellbeing, water quality, and biodiversity. The results of such practices were clear in soil corruption, loss of dirt, and the decay of fundamental pollinators like honey bees.

To address these difficulties and shift toward a more feasible and capable way to deal with food creation and utilization, the significance of neighborhood food obtaining started to acquire noticeable quality. Nearby food obtaining includes the creation, dispersion, and utilization of food inside a characterized geological region, frequently revolved around a neighborhood local area or district. This approach focuses on short inventory chains, where the distance between the wellspring of food and the buyer is limited.

The reception of neighborhood food obtaining significantly affects how we might interpret food. It restores the association among individuals and their food, making a more straightforward and responsible food framework. Shoppers are progressively ready to know where their food comes from, the way things are created, and who is answerable for its development. This straightforwardness has prompted a restored trust in the food store network.

One of the critical principles of nearby food obtaining is the accentuation on new, occasional produce. Nearby food is frequently collected at its pinnacle readiness and eaten before long, protecting the flavors, healthy benefit, and newness of the produce. Interestingly, the globalized food framework frequently depends on long haul stockpiling, refrigeration, and transportation, which can prompt the deficiency of flavor and nourishing quality.

The idea of "ranch to-table" has become vital to neighborhood food obtaining. Eateries and purchasers the same have embraced obtaining their food straightforwardly from nearby homesteads and makers. This training has prompted the improvement of solid connections among customers and nearby ranchers, encouraging a feeling of local area and trust. The special interaction between food makers and buyers has revived an appreciation for the people who work to take care of us.

Neighborhood food obtaining has likewise assumed a critical part in renewing nearby economies. As purchasers focus on neighborhood items, interest for territorially developed and delivered food has expanded. This, thus, has prompted the production of new positions, especially in cultivating, food handling, and dissemination. Limited scope ranchers, food craftsmans, and nearby organizations have encountered development and achievement.

Besides, the shift toward nearby food obtaining advances a more evenhanded dissemination of abundance inside networks. By supporting nearby ranchers and food makers, shoppers assist with guaranteeing that the financial advantages of food creation stay inside the district, as opposed to being piped to huge agribusinesses or far off enterprises. This monetary reallocation reinforces nearby economies and improves local area flexibility.

The hug of neighborhood food obtaining has additionally had critical natural advantages. Shortening the distance food makes a trip from homestead to plate lessens the carbon impression of our feasts. Lower ozone harming substance discharges result from less significant distance transportation, and the utilization of food that is developed nearer to home altogether decreases the ecological effect related with the worldwide food production network.

Also, nearby food obtaining frequently advances feasible agrarian practices. Limited scope and nearby ranchers are more disposed to utilize regenerative horticulture methods, for example, crop pivot, cover trimming, and the utilization of regular composts. These practices assist with further developing soil wellbeing, increment biodiversity, and decrease the dependence on manufactured synthetic compounds. Conversely, huge scope modern farming has been a significant supporter of soil debasement and water contamination.

Chasing neighborhood food obtaining, there has been a resurgence of interest in treasure and legacy crop assortments. These exceptional and various harvests, which had been minimized in the time of modern horticulture, have reappeared as fundamental parts of neighborhood food frameworks. Their conservation keeps up with hereditary variety inside the food supply, which is basic notwithstanding environmental change and pandemics.

As neighborhood food frameworks embrace the variety of treasure and legacy crops, they likewise will generally consolidate a more extensive scope of plant species. Various yield turns, intercropping, and agroforestry have become normal practices. This approach has made stronger and biodiverse biological systems, upgrading the manageability of agribusiness.

The shift toward neighborhood food obtaining reaches out past yields to the animals business. Nearby and local animals cultivating has acquired conspicuousness, with an emphasis on bringing creatures up in empathetic and feasible circumstances. Because of worries about animal government assistance and natural effect, guidelines and customer inclinations have moved from production line ranches to fed and grass-took care of animals.

Moral and supportable practices in the meat and dairy industry have become key to the neighborhood food obtaining development. This shift has not just better the nature of meat and dairy items however has likewise added to the government assistance of creatures, diminishing the antagonistic effects of enormous scope domesticated animals creation.

The accentuation on feasible and compassionate cultivating rehearses has prompted the reinforcing of guidelines inside the meat and dairy industry. State run administrations and networks have forced stricter principles to guarantee the moral treatment of animals and lessen the natural effect of huge scope domesticated animals cultivating.

The significance of nearby food obtaining isn't bound to explicit locales or nations; it has developed into a worldwide peculiarity. Different districts of the world have adjusted and embraced neighborhood food obtaining in novel ways, frequently mirroring their social, ecological, and financial settings.

In Europe, for example, nearby food obtaining has revived an appreciation for customary agrarian practices and culinary legacy. Nations like Italy and France have commended the utilization of new, occasional fixings in their food for a really long time. Nearby business sectors, known as "ranchers' business sectors," have kept on flourishing as energetic centers of movement, where purchasers can interface straightforwardly with neighborhood makers and craftsmans.

In the US, the neighborhood food development has picked up speed across assorted districts. Ranchers' business sectors, local area upheld farming (CSA) programs, and metropolitan nurseries have become essential parts of the food scene. Shoppers have embraced knowing their ranchers and food makers by and by, which cultivates a feeling of trust and local area.

In Asia, neighborhood food obtaining has revived customary cultivating rehearses and culinary practices. Rice paddies, terraced farming, and various editing frameworks have made a resurgence. The fastidious consideration taken in developing rice and other staple harvests, joined with the utilization of neighborhood and occasional fixings, has prompted another appreciation for Asian food.

The significance of nearby food obtaining in Africa has brought about the reception of dry season safe yields like millet and sorghum. Local area based agribusiness and cooperatives have engaged nearby ranchers to take care of their networks while saving normal assets.

South America has embraced its rich culinary practices while rethinking its old food culture with a cutting edge bend. Nearby business sectors, known as "souks," stay energetic centers of action, displaying the freshest fixings and saving culinary legacy.

In the polar districts, the impacts of environmental change have been generally articulated. Creative ways to deal with food creation have arisen, including the utilization of nurseries and hydroponics frameworks to empower the all year development of new produce. Networks have adjusted to new food frameworks, utilizing environmentally friendly power sources and maintainable fishing practices to guarantee food security.

3.2 Benefits for farmers and consumers

The shift towards privately obtained and new food has achieved a huge number of advantages for the two ranchers and shoppers. This change of our food frameworks has made a cooperative relationship where each party receives the benefits of a more reasonable and straightforward way to deal with food creation and utilization.

For ranchers, the shift to neighborhood food obtaining has been especially extraordinary. Limited scope ranchers, specifically, have encountered a resurgence in their jobs as they assume a focal part in these confined food frameworks. The advantages for ranchers are complex and go past financial benefits.

One of the main advantages for ranchers is the expanded market open doors and interest for their produce. In the globalized food framework, limited scope ranchers frequently attempted to rival enormous agribusinesses that overwhelmed the market. The sheer size of modern horticulture implied that little ranchers experienced issues arriving at an expansive purchaser base.

Nearby food obtaining has changed this dynamic. As shoppers focus on privately developed and delivered food, limited scope ranchers end up in a situation to supply new, occasional produce straightforwardly to neighborhood networks. Ranchers' business sectors, local area upheld horticulture (CSA) programs, and direct-to-customer deals have become essential parts of nearby food frameworks.

These immediate showcasing channels permit ranchers to hold a bigger piece of the benefits from their deals. Rather than offering their produce to mediators or huge enterprises, they can associate straightforwardly with shoppers. This immediate relationship has worked on ranchers' pay as well as encouraged a feeling of local area and trust among makers and customers.

Also, nearby food obtaining has set out open doors for expanded crop creation. Limited scope ranchers can grow a more extensive assortment of harvests that are appropriate to their neighborhood surroundings and shopper inclinations.

This variety takes into account crop pivot and intercropping, which are known to further develop soil wellbeing and lessen the gamble of bug pervasions. The advantages of these practices stretch out to the two ranchers and the climate.

Manageable rural practices, like regenerative farming, have become vital to neighborhood food frameworks. These practices focus on soil wellbeing, biodiversity, and the utilization of normal manures. Ranchers who embrace these methods lessen their ecological effect as well as make stronger and useful rural scenes.

The shift to neighborhood food obtaining has likewise prompted a resurgence of interest in legacy and legacy crop assortments. Limited scope ranchers play had a critical impact in saving these novel and different harvests. As buyers become more mindful of the significance of keeping up with hereditary variety in our food supply, the interest for these harvests has expanded. This has permitted ranchers to take part in the conservation of rural legacy while furnishing buyers with a more extensive assortment of new, occasional produce.

Moreover, nearby food frameworks frequently advance moral and practical animals cultivating. Ranchers who raise animals for meat or dairy inside these frameworks are urged to utilize accommodating and manageable practices. The accentuation on animal government assistance and natural effect has brought about additional moral and maintainable cultivating techniques.

As customers become more aware of the treatment of animals and the ecological effect of domesticated animals cultivating, limited scope ranchers have adjusted to live up to these assumptions. Guidelines and purchaser inclinations have moved away from plant cultivating and enormous scope activities, empowering the reception of fed and grass-took care of domesticated animals cultivating. This progress benefits the two ranchers and buyers.

In the meat and dairy industry, moral and manageable practices have become fundamental to the neighborhood food obtaining development. Ranchers who raise animals in additional others conscious and normal circumstances not just work on the nature of their meat and dairy items yet in addition add to the government assistance of the animals and diminish the unfavorable effects of enormous scope animals creation.

To guarantee the moral treatment of animals and diminish the natural effect of domesticated animals cultivating, state run administrations and networks have forced stricter guidelines inside the meat and dairy industry. This has safeguarded animal government assistance as well as assisted ranchers with changing to additional manageable works on, guaranteeing the suitability of their tasks over the long haul.

The financial advantages of nearby food obtaining reach out to neighborhood food craftsmans and private ventures. Nearby food makers, like cooks, cheesemakers, and art refreshment producers, have encountered development and outcome in this new food scene.

As customers look for superior grade, privately delivered things, these craftsmans have earned respect and piece of the pie.

Also, the restoration of neighborhood food frameworks has prompted financial reallocation inside networks. Rather than benefits from food creation being piped to enormous agribusinesses or far off companies, a greater amount of the financial advantages stay inside the locale. The help of neighborhood ranchers and food makers adds to the versatility and financial security of nearby networks.

For shoppers, the advantages of nearby food obtaining are similarly huge. This shift has essentially changed how individuals see, buy, and devour food, bringing about a scope of benefits for their prosperity, the climate, and their networks.

One of the most prompt advantages for purchasers is the superior nature of their food. Neighborhood food is frequently gathered at the pinnacle of readiness and eaten before long, protecting the flavors, dietary benefit, and newness of the produce. The more limited distance between the wellspring of food and the customer's plate guarantees that the time-touchy characteristics of food are held.

Conversely, the globalized food framework depends on significant distance transportation, which frequently requires the utilization of long haul stockpiling, refrigeration, and transportation techniques. These cycles can prompt a deficiency of flavor and healthful quality, bringing about food that is less new and less delightful.

The idea of "ranch to-table" has become vital to nearby food obtaining. Eateries and purchasers the same have embraced obtaining their food straightforwardly from neighborhood homesteads and makers. This training has revived an appreciation for the people who work to take care of us, and it has encouraged a feeling of trust and local area.

Customers likewise benefit from expanded straightforwardness in the nearby food framework. As they look to comprehend where their food comes from, the way things are delivered, and who is liable for its development, they have a more prominent enthusiasm for the starting points of their food. This straightforwardness engages shoppers to settle on informed decisions about the food they buy and eat, encouraging a more profound association with their dinners.

The unique interaction between food makers and shoppers significantly affects the manner in which individuals see and worth their food. Shoppers are bound to put resources into the nearby food framework, realizing that their buys straightforwardly support their neighborhood networks and the people who produce their food. This feeling of association has revived a more profound appreciation for the ranchers and food craftsmans who work tenaciously to give new, quality food.

As far as wellbeing, the advantages of neighborhood food obtaining are huge. With a reestablished accentuation on new, natural food sources, shoppers are bound to eat a more extensive assortment of products of the soil, contingent upon occasional accessibility. This dietary change has prompted a lessening in diet-related medical problems, like weight and coronary illness.

The decrease in handled food sources in the nearby food framework has likewise added to better eating regimens. Individuals are bound to consume natural, new fixings, decreasing their admission of counterfeit added substances, additives, and unfortunate fats. This has prompted a decrease in way of life related medical conditions, which frequently result from the utilization of handled and vigorously changed food sources.

The accentuation on the healthy benefit of new, natural food sources has changed the manner in which individuals view their weight control plans. They have come to comprehend that food can be both medication and food. This acknowledgment has prompted an all encompassing way to deal with prosperity and an acknowledgment that the nature of the food they devour straightforwardly affects their wellbeing and imperativeness.

Past wellbeing, nearby food obtaining significantly affects the climate. By shortening the distance food goes from homestead to plate, the carbon impression of dinners is altogether diminished. This is pivotal notwithstanding mounting proof of the outcomes of environmental change.

Lower ozone harming substance outflows result from less significant distance transportation of food, prompting a decrease in the ecological effect related with the worldwide food store network. Customers are progressively mindful of the association between their food decisions and environmental change, which has prompted more eco-cognizant dietary choices.

The decrease of ozone harming substance outflows is especially critical given the desperation of tending to environmental change. The ecological effect of the globalized food framework was difficult to overlook, as food went tremendous distances to arrive at shoppers, devouring critical measures of energy and assets. The neighborhood food obtaining development has given a fundamental answer for alleviate these adverse consequences.

The natural advantages of neighborhood food obtaining are not restricted to diminished fossil fuel byproducts. Limited scope ranchers who utilize manageable agrarian practices inside these frameworks make stronger environments. Various yield turns, intercropping, and agroforestry have become normal practices. This approach has further developed soil wellbeing, increment biodiversity, and diminish the dependence on engineered synthetic compounds, which are all fundamental for supportable farming.

The restoration of customary cultivating rehearses, like rice paddies, terraced horticulture, and various editing frameworks, has added to a resurgence of rural legacy and biodiversity. This has been especially obvious in Asia, where fastidious consideration in developing rice and other staple yields, joined with the utilization of nearby and occasional fixings, has prompted another appreciation for Asian cooking.

Notwithstanding manageability, the nearby food obtaining development has encouraged a feeling of local area and social obligation. Shoppers who focus on privately obtained food are much of the time more participated in their nearby networks and more associated with their neighbors. This has prompted a resurgence of local area based farming and a more profound appreciation for the people who produce our food.

The development of nearby food frameworks has set out financial open doors inside networks, which has the expanding influence of helping neighborhood economies and diminishing pay disparity. The monetary advantages of nearby food obtaining stretch out to private companies and craftsmans, who have encountered development and progress in this new food scene.

One of the most convincing parts of the neighborhood food obtaining development is its accentuation on moral and maintainable practices. Customers have become more mindful of the treatment of animals and the natural effect of domesticated animals cultivating, which has prompted a shift away from plant cultivating and enormous scope tasks.

Ranchers and purchasers the same have embraced more moral and maintainable animals cultivating rehearses. The accentuation on animal government assistance and the climate has brought about additional compassionate and practical cultivating strategies, which benefit the two ranchers and shoppers.

In general, the shift towards privately obtained and new food has prompted various advantages for ranchers and purchasers. It has renewed limited scope cultivating, set out financial open doors inside networks, worked on the quality and newness of food, encouraged a more profound association among makers and buyers, and added to better weight control plans. Furthermore, the decrease of ozone depleting substance discharges and the reception of supportable agrarian practices have made positive natural impacts. This change in our food frameworks addresses an essential change in values, focusing on maintainability, wellbeing, and local area over comfort and cost. As we keep on embracing the significance of neighborhood food obtaining, we perceive that our food decisions straightforwardly affect the prosperity of the planet and the thriving of people in the future.

Chapter 4

Minimally Processed Foods

The idea of negligibly handled food sources has built up some forward momentum as of late as buyers and specialists the same perceive the possible advantages of getting away from intensely handled and exceptionally refined items. This shift addresses a key change in the manner we ponder and communicate with the food we devour. In this investigation of negligibly handled food sources, we will dig into the meaning of such food varieties, their benefits, and the ramifications they hold for our wellbeing, climate, and by and large prosperity.

Negligibly handled food sources, frequently alluded to as "genuine food varieties," are things that have gone through insignificant change from their regular state. These food varieties are commonly entire and pure, with almost no added substances, additives, or counterfeit fixings. All things considered, they mirror the straightforwardness and immaculateness of their normal structure, making them all the more firmly lined up with what nature gives.

At the center of negligibly handled food sources is protecting the uprightness of the first fixings. This implies that natural products, vegetables, grains, nuts, seeds, lean proteins, and natural dairy are viewed as negligibly handled when they are consumed without huge change. For instance, an entire apple, a sack of unroasted nuts, or a new filet of fish fall into this class.

Nonetheless, it's critical to take note of that insignificant handling can likewise incorporate specific techniques that improve food handling and safeguarding without compromising the food's dietary benefit. Models incorporate purification, freezing, drying, and maturation. In these cases, the point is to broaden the time span of usability of the food while holding its fundamental characteristics.

Insignificantly handled food sources balance strongly with vigorously handled things, like sweet oats, microwaveable suppers, and exceptionally refined snacks. These handled food varieties frequently contain a considerable rundown of added substances, including fake flavors, varieties, additives, and sugars, a significant number of which are hard to articulate and comprehend.

The upsides of picking insignificantly handled food varieties are various and influence different parts of our lives, including our wellbeing, the climate, and our relationship with food.

Negligibly handled food sources, first and foremost, will generally be more supplement thick. This implies they give a higher grouping of fundamental nutrients, minerals, and other helpful mixtures per calorie contrasted with intensely handled food sources. For instance, a new, entire apple is wealthy in fiber, cell reinforcements, and fundamental supplements, while apple-seasoned lunch rooms frequently contain added sugars and less wellbeing advancing parts.

The regular effortlessness of negligibly handled food varieties can essentially add to a decent and solid eating regimen. Devouring these food sources gives an under-pinning of supplements that our bodies need to ideally work. This can prompt better energy levels, further developed assimilation, and improved in general prosperity.

Notwithstanding their nourishing advantages, negligibly handled food sources are much of the time lower in added sugars, unfortunate fats, and over the top salt, which are normal guilty parties behind many eating regimen related medical problems, including heftiness, diabetes, and coronary illness. The shortfall of unreasonable added substances and additives in negligibly handled food varieties implies that shoppers have more command over what they put into their bodies, making it simpler to go with wellbeing cognizant decisions.

Negligibly handled food varieties additionally line up with standards of careful and instinctive eating. By picking food varieties that are nearer to their normal state, people can all the more likely adjust themselves to their appetite and completion prompts. This assists cultivate a better relationship with food, as well as a more noteworthy consciousness of one's body and its necessities.

One more critical benefit of negligibly handled food varieties is their part in supporting economical and harmless to the ecosystem food frameworks. Exceptionally handled food varieties frequently depend on asset concentrated techniques, for example, huge scope monoculture cultivating and broad transportation organizations, which can add to natural debasement and asset exhaustion.

Negligibly handled food varieties, then again, are frequently connected with nearby and limited scope cultivating. This diminishes the ecological effect of food creation, as it frequently requires less assets, less energy, and produces less ozone harming substance emanations.

Negligibly handled food varieties additionally will generally include less bundling and waste, further adding to manageability.

The advancement of nearby, negligibly handled food sources can prompt more noteworthy local area commitment and backing for neighborhood horticulture. This can possibly strengthen nearby economies, give more monetary open doors to little ranchers, and decrease the carbon impression of the food store network. Supporting neighborhood farming cultivates a feeling of local area and fortifies the association among customers and the wellsprings of their food.

Moreover, insignificantly handled food sources frequently reducedly affect food-related medical problems, for example, weight and diabetes, which can put a critical weight on medical services frameworks. By advancing the utilization of food sources that are normally energizing, social orders might encounter a lessening in diet-related medical issues, prompting decreased medical care costs and worked on generally general wellbeing.

The expanded interest for negligibly handled food sources has likewise prompted a developing business sector for these items, which can uphold private companies and food craftsmans. This is especially apparent in the ascent of nearby ranchers' business sectors, where buyers can straightforwardly buy new, pure produce and backing neighborhood ranchers and makers.

Moreover, the shift towards negligibly handled food varieties can move people to foster their culinary abilities and take part in home cooking. This not just considers more prominent imagination in the kitchen yet in addition gives a chance to all the more likely comprehend the fixings that go into the food we eat.

Eating negligibly handled food varieties can advance a more grounded feeling of food security and independence. By focusing on nearby and entire food sources, people become less subject to exceptionally handled and frequently less nutritious things. This confidence can give a feeling of strengthening and diminish weakness to store network interruptions.

While the benefits of negligibly handled food varieties are various, it's essential to recognize that they are not without difficulties and contemplations. One of the essential worries is openness. For certain people, getting to new, negligibly handled food sources can be testing, especially in regions where these choices are restricted or cost-restrictive.

In many examples, profoundly handled and less nutritious food sources are more promptly accessible and more affordable than negligibly handled choices. This can make abberations in admittance to better food decisions, known as food deserts, which excessively influence low-pay networks.

Resolving issues of food access and moderateness is fundamental to guarantee that the advantages of negligibly handled food varieties are available to all. Networks, policymakers, and associations should cooperate to make evenhanded food frameworks that focus on wellbeing and manageability, especially in underserved regions.

Another thought is comfort. Vigorously handled food sources frequently take care of occupied ways of life, offering speedy and simple feast arrangements. The time and exertion expected for feast arranging and cooking with negligibly handled fixings can be an obstruction for certain people.

Nonetheless, this challenge can be tended to through instruction and the advancement of culinary abilities. By showing people how to plan straightforward, nutritious dinners utilizing negligibly handled fixings, we can engage them to settle on better food decisions without forfeiting comfort.

The discernment that insignificantly handled food varieties are less tasty or charming than their vigorously handled partners can likewise be an impediment for certain customers. In any case, this discernment is much of the time in light of commonality and openness. As individuals become more familiar with the normal kinds of entire food varieties, their palates might adjust, prompting a more prominent appreciation for the taste and assortment that insignificantly handled food sources offer.

Another worry is the timeframe of realistic usability of negligibly handled food varieties. Since they miss the mark on additives and added substances normally found in vigorously handled items, they might have a more limited timeframe of realistic usability and require more continuous restocking. In any case, this challenge can be tended to through appropriate capacity, feast arranging, and decreased food squander.

The advanced food industry frequently intensely advertises exceptionally handled food sources, making them effectively open and enticing for buyers. To empower the reception of insignificantly handled food sources, training and mindfulness crusades are fundamental. These missions can advance the dietary and natural advantages of insignificantly handled food varieties and give direction on the most proficient method to integrate them into day to day slims down.

Schools and local area associations can assume a fundamental part in showing kids and grown-ups the significance of negligibly handled food sources. Cooking classes, cultivating projects, and nourishment schooling can assist people with fostering the abilities and information expected to pursue better food decisions.

Policymakers likewise play a basic part to play in supporting and boosting the creation and utilization of negligibly handled food sources. This should be possible through drives like appropriations for nearby ranchers, the advancement of ranchers' business sectors, and guidelines that advance food marking straightforwardness.

Also, policymakers can attempt to decrease the promoting and accessibility of vigorously handled food sources, especially in schools and public spaces. Tax collection arrangements can be utilized to put the utilization of sweet refreshments and tidbits down, while at the same time financing nourishment schooling and better food choices.

4.1 The impact of food processing on health

Food handling is a complicated and diverse part of the cutting edge food framework, with far reaching influences on our wellbeing. The expression "food handling" incorporates a wide range of exercises, from cleaning and arranging to cooking, protecting, and bundling. While food handling has gotten many advantages terms of accommodation, time span of usability, and openness, it additionally brings up basic issues about what these cycles mean for the nourishing quality and generally empowerment of the food varieties we eat.

The effect of food handling on wellbeing is a subject of huge worry, as it assumes a vital part in forming dietary examples, nourishing substance, and the pervasiveness of diet-related medical problems. In this investigation, we will dig into the different manners by which food handling impacts wellbeing, examining both the positive and negative viewpoints, and looking at how customers can go with informed decisions to keep a decent and wellbeing cognizant eating regimen.

Food handling can meaningfully affect the wholesome substance of the food sources we devour. Understanding these impacts is fundamental for pursuing informed dietary decisions.

Constructive outcomes of Food Handling on Sustenance:

Protection of Supplements: Some food handling techniques, for example, canning, freezing, and drying, can really save the dietary substance of food varieties. These strategies can expand the time span of usability of transient things and make them accessible all year, guaranteeing that fundamental supplements stay available.

Fortress: now and again, food handling incorporates the expansion of supplements to upgrade the nourishing profile of the item. Normal models incorporate the fortress of cereals and grains with nutrients and minerals, for example, folic corrosive, iron, and B nutrients, which can assist with tending to supplement lacks in specific populaces.

Upgraded Absorbability: Cooking and intensity handling can work on the edibility of specific food sources. For instance, cooking can separate the cell walls of plant-based food varieties, making their supplements all the more promptly accessible for retention in the human stomach related framework.

Decrease of Enemies of Supplements: Certain food handling methods, like drenching and maturation, can assist with lessening enemies of supplements, normally happening intensifies that restrain the retention of supplements. For example, the maturation of soybeans to deliver soy sauce and miso can separate phytic corrosive, a typical enemy of supplement.

Expanded Accessibility of Occasional Food varieties: Food handling takes into consideration the safeguarding and accessibility of occasional food sources over time. This can upgrade dietary variety and admittance to a more extensive scope of supplements.

Adverse consequences of Food Handling on Sustenance:

Supplement Misfortune: The handling of food sources, especially through techniques, for example, canning, freezing, and getting dried out, can bring about the deficiency of specific intensity touchy supplements, like L-ascorbic acid and some B nutrients. Broadened capacity and cooking times can worsen these misfortunes.

Obliteration of Compounds: Food handling, particularly when exposed to high intensity, can annihilate proteins normally present in crude food sources. These proteins assume a part in processing and supplement retention. For example, heat treatment can deactivate proteins in crude products of the soil.

Added Sugars and Salt: Many handled food sources are loaded down with added sugars and salt, which can unfavorably affect wellbeing. Unreasonable sugar utilization is connected to stoutness, diabetes, and dental issues, while high salt admission is related with hypertension and coronary illness.

Refined Carbs: Food handling frequently includes the refining of grains, like wheat, to make items like white bread and pasta. During this refining system, the external wheat and internal microorganism layers of the grain are eliminated, alongside fundamental supplements and dietary fiber.

Trans Fats: Incomplete hydrogenation, a food handling strategy used to harden fluid oils, can prompt the development of trans fats. Trans fats are known to expand the gamble of coronary illness and other medical problems.

Loss of Fiber: Handling can bring about the expulsion of dietary fiber from food varieties. Fiber is significant for stomach related wellbeing and has various advantages, including advancing satiety and decreasing the gamble of constant sicknesses.

The Effect of Food Handling on Dietary Examples:

The omnipresence of exceptionally handled food varieties has altogether modified dietary examples around the world. The comfort and long timeframe of realistic usability of these food varieties have added to their far and wide utilization, frequently to the detriment of a more adjusted and wellbeing cognizant eating regimen.

Expanded Utilization of Super Handled Food sources: Super handled food varieties, like sweet cereals, cheap food, and exceptionally refined snacks, have become staples in many eating regimens. These things are regularly energy-thick however supplement poor, prompting exorbitant calorie admission and expected supplement inadequacies.

High Sugar Admission: Food handling is firmly connected with the expansion of sugars to a great many items. Unnecessary sugar utilization is a main pressing issue, as it is connected to the rising pervasiveness of weight, type 2 diabetes, and dental issues.

Overconsumption of Sodium: Handled food varieties frequently contain elevated degrees of added salt, which can add to raised circulatory strain, hypertension, and an expanded gamble of coronary illness.

Imbalanced Macronutrient Proportions: Exceptionally handled food varieties are oftentimes high in refined carbs and undesirable fats, prompting imbalanced macronutrient proportions in consumes less calories. Such irregular characteristics can add to weight and other eating routine related medical problems.

Decreased Admission of New, Entire Food varieties: The prepared accessibility of handled food sources can diminish the utilization of new, entire food varieties, including natural products, vegetables, and entire grains. These food sources are wealthy in fundamental supplements and dietary fiber, which are significant for generally speaking wellbeing.

Twisted Piece Sizes: Exceptionally handled food varieties are many times divided in a manner that energizes gorging. The "supersizing" of inexpensive food dinners and the promoting of huge tidbit bundles can add to unreasonable calorie admission.

The Job of Food Handling in the Pervasiveness of Diet-Related Medical problems:

The boundless utilization of exceptionally handled food sources has added to a worldwide wellbeing emergency portrayed by diet-related medical problems. Understanding the job of food handling in the predominance of these issues is fundamental for tending to and alleviating their effect.

Heftiness: Exceptionally handled food sources are habitually high in calories, added sugars, and unfortunate fats, which can prompt gorging and weight gain. The energy thickness of these food sources makes it simple to devour abundance calories without feeling full.

Type 2 Diabetes: The utilization of food sources wealthy in added sugars and refined starches can prompt insulin opposition, a forerunner to type 2 diabetes. The quick processing of these food varieties brings about fluctuating glucose levels and an expanded gamble of diabetes.

Cardiovascular Sickness: Diets high in handled food sources, especially those containing trans fats, exorbitant salt, and added sugars, are related with an expanded gamble of coronary illness. These food sources can add to raised pulse, aggravation, and atherosclerosis.

Dental Issues: Profoundly handled food sources, particularly sweet bites and refreshments, are impeding to oral wellbeing. Sugar utilization is an essential driver of dental caries and tooth rot.

Gastrointestinal Issues: The expulsion of dietary fiber from handled food sources can prompt stomach related issues, including stoppage and diverticular infection.

Supplement Lacks: The unreasonable utilization of handled food varieties can uproot supplement rich entire food sources in the eating routine, possibly prompting supplement inadequacies.

Persistent Irritation: Profoundly handled food sources can advance ongoing aggravation, which is related with different medical problems, including corpulence, coronary illness, and immune system conditions.

The Effect of Food Handling on Mental Parts of Eating:

Notwithstanding the actual wellbeing suggestions, food handling can impact mental parts of eating, including food inclinations, desires, and habit-forming conduct.

Food Satisfactoriness: The handling of food sources frequently includes the expansion of sugar, salt, and unfortunate fats to upgrade flavor and attractiveness. This can make exceptionally handled food sources seriously engaging and fulfilling, possibly prompting overconsumption.

Food Enslavement: A few exceptionally handled food sources, especially those high in added sugars and undesirable fats, can set off habit-forming eating ways of behaving. These food sources enact reward focuses in the cerebrum, prompting desires and gorging.

Food Desires: The regular utilization of handled food varieties can prompt desires for sweet and pungent flavors, making it trying to embrace a more adjusted and well-being cognizant eating regimen.

Tangible Over-burden: Vigorously handled food varieties are frequently intended to give an extraordinary tactile encounter, with dynamic tones, solid flavors, and interesting surfaces. These tangible qualities can desensitize taste buds and make normal, natural food sources appear to be boring by examination.

4.2 The shift towards minimally processed products

The shift towards negligibly handled items has turned into a huge and groundbreaking pattern in the domain of food utilization and creation. In reality as we know it where profoundly handled, comfort situated food varieties have long ruled the market, this shift addresses a key change in the manner we ponder our eating regimens and the food sources we eat. In this investigation of negligibly handled items, we will dive into the meaning of these food sources, the explanations for the pattern, and the various benefits they proposition to purchasers, ranchers, and the climate.

Insignificantly handled items, frequently alluded to as "genuine food varieties" or "entire food sources," are those that have gone through negligible modification from their normal state. They are commonly basic and pure, with practically zero added substances, additives, or fake fixings. All things considered, they intently look like the regular type of the fixings from which they are determined.

At the core of insignificantly handled items is protecting the intrinsic characteristics and uprightness of the first fixings. This implies that natural products, vegetables, grains, nuts, seeds, lean proteins, and natural dairy items can be viewed as insignificantly handled when they are consumed with negligible adjustment. For instance, an entire apple, a pack of unroasted nuts, or a new cut of unseasoned fish are instances of insignificantly handled items.

Nonetheless, it's critical to take note of that insignificant handling can likewise incorporate specific techniques that upgrade sanitation and conservation without altogether adjusting the food's healthy benefit. These strategies incorporate sanitization, freezing, drying, and aging, all of which mean to expand the timeframe of realistic usability of the food while holding its fundamental characteristics.

The shift towards negligibly handled items is driven by a mix of elements that answer the changing inclinations and necessities of purchasers, as well as more extensive worries about wellbeing, manageability, and the climate.

Healthful Cognizance: Customers are progressively mindful of the dietary benefit of the food sources they eat. They look for items that are wealthy in fundamental supplements and liberated from fake added substances, overabundance sugar, undesirable fats, and extreme salt. Negligibly handled items are viewed as a method for adjusting diets to wellbeing cognizant objectives.

Straightforwardness and Trust: The longing for straightforwardness in the food store network has developed altogether. Customers need to know where their food comes from, the way things are delivered, and what fixings it contains. Insignificantly handled items frequently give more straightforwardness, as they are nearer to their normal source.

Wellbeing and Way of life Decisions: Wellbeing and health patterns have prodded an interest in negligibly handled items. These food varieties are viewed as a method for supporting different dietary inclinations and ways of life, like veggie lover, vegetarian, paleo, and natural eating regimens.

Manageability and Neighborhood Obtaining: There is a developing accentuation on maintainability and harmless to the ecosystem food frameworks. Insignificantly handled items are frequently connected with nearby and limited scope cultivating, diminishing the natural effect of food creation and transportation.

Food Quality and Flavor: Insignificantly handled items are esteemed for their flavor and newness. Shoppers are progressively keen on encountering the regular taste of fixings without the obstruction of counterfeit flavors and added substances.

Sanitation: The insignificant handling of food sources can improve food handling. For example, purification and controlled climate capacity can assist with lessening the gamble of foodborne ailments.

Social and Culinary Customs: Numerous culinary practices and societies have long embraced negligibly handled food varieties. The restoration and festivity of these practices have added to the resurgence of insignificantly handled items.

The benefits of picking insignificantly handled items are various and influence different parts of our lives, including our wellbeing, the climate, and our association with food sources.

Medical advantages:

Supplement Thickness: Negligibly handled items are many times more supplement thick, meaning they give a higher grouping of fundamental nutrients, minerals, and gainful mixtures per calorie contrasted with profoundly handled food sources. For example, new leafy foods are plentiful in nutrients, cell reinforcements, and dietary fiber.

Diminished Added Sugars and Salt: Profoundly handled food sources are frequently loaded down with added sugars and salt, which can add to eat less carbs related medical problems, like stoutness, diabetes, and coronary illness. Insignificantly handled items will generally have lower levels of these unsafe added substances.

Entire Grains: Negligibly handled items, like entire grains, contain the whole grain piece, which gives fundamental supplements and dietary fiber. This is as opposed to refined grains, which are deprived of their wheat and microorganism layers, bringing about a deficiency of supplements and fiber.

Newness and Flavor: Insignificantly handled items are known for their newness and flavor. Devouring food sources at their pinnacle readiness considers a prevalent taste insight and higher satisfaction in dinners.

Straightforwardness and Trust: Negligibly handled items frequently give an immediate connection among purchasers and food sources. This encourages trust and a feeling of association, as shoppers have a more clear comprehension of where their food comes from and the way things are created.

Natural Advantages:

Manageable Cultivating Practices: Negligibly handled items are frequently connected with nearby and limited scope cultivating, which will in general utilize more supportable rural practices. This can incorporate yield pivot, decreased manufactured substance use, and further developed soil wellbeing.

Decreased Carbon Impression: The more limited distance that negligibly handled items head out from ranch to table lessens the carbon impression of dinners. Less dependence on significant distance transportation and refrigeration mitigates the ecological effect of the food production network.

Decrease of Food Squander: Negligibly handled items ordinarily include less bundling and waste contrasted with profoundly handled things. This diminishes the in general natural effect of food creation.

Neighborhood Food Frameworks: The advancement of nearby and insignificantly handled items can prompt more prominent local area commitment and backing for neighborhood farming. This can possibly empower neighborhood economies, give more monetary open doors to little ranchers, and lessen the carbon impression of the food store network.

Culinary and Social Advantages:

Food Variety: Negligibly handled items empower dietary variety by offering admittance to new, occasional fixings. This can prompt a more extensive scope of flavors and culinary encounters.

Culinary Imagination: Getting ready feasts with insignificantly handled fixings considers more prominent culinary innovativeness and trial and error. Home cooks have the amazing chance to investigate assorted cooking methods and flavor blends.

Association with Culinary Customs: The utilization of negligibly handled items frequently lines up with social and culinary practices that have commended the regular flavors and characteristics of elements for ages. This association with legacy adds profundity and importance to feasts.

The shift towards negligibly handled items is likewise altering the manner in which we approach sanitation and foodborne ailments. While the advantages of negligibly handled items are various, there are contemplations and difficulties that should be addressed to guarantee their security.

Sanitation and Insignificantly Handled Items:

Chance of Defilement: Insignificantly handled items, particularly those like new produce and crude nuts, may convey a gamble of tainting with microbes, like E. coli or Salmonella. This chance is limited through safe dealing with, stockpiling, and rural practices.

Safe Taking care of and Cleanliness: Shoppers should be instructed on safe dealing with rehearses for negligibly handled items. Washing products of the soil completely, putting away things at the right temperature, and following legitimate food handling strategies are fundamental.

Guidelines and Oversight: States and sanitation organizations should assume a part in laying out guidelines and oversight to guarantee the wellbeing of negligibly handled items. This incorporates checking rural practices, creation offices, and conveyance organizations.

Shopper Mindfulness: Customer familiarity with food handling is urgent. Shoppers ought to be educated about the potential dangers related with negligibly handled items and how to limit those dangers through safe food taking care of practices.

Nearby Obtaining and Discernibility: An emphasis on neighborhood obtaining and detectability can upgrade sanitation for insignificantly handled items. Knowing the wellspring of the food and the creation techniques utilized can increment trust in its wellbeing.

The shift towards negligibly handled items addresses a tremendous change in the manner we ponder our eating regimens and the food sources we eat. While this change accompanies many advantages, it's essential to address difficulties connected with access, reasonableness, and wellbeing to guarantee that these benefits are open to all people and networks.

4.3 Examples of minimally processed foods

Insignificantly handled food sources, otherwise called "genuine food varieties" or "entire food varieties," are those that go through negligible modification from their regular state, holding their innate characteristics and dietary benefit. These food varieties are valued for their straightforwardness and virtue, making them a significant piece of a reasonable and wellbeing cognizant eating routine. In this investigation, we will dig into instances of negligibly handled food varieties across different food classes, from leafy foods to grains, meats, and dairy items.

Products of the soil:

Entire Natural products: New organic products like apples, bananas, oranges, and berries are incredible instances of insignificantly handled food sources. They are consumed in their regular state with practically no change. Entire natural products are plentiful in nutrients, minerals, dietary fiber, and cell reinforcements.

Vegetable Mixture: A variety of negligibly handled vegetables, like carrots, celery, and chime peppers, can be served crude as a crunchy and nutritious tidbit. These vegetables are in many cases cut into advantageous scaled down pieces.

Salad Greens: Blended salad greens, including lettuce, spinach, and arugula, are negligibly handled items. They are normally washed and bundled for comfort, protecting their regular newness.

New Cut Vegetables: Pre-cut vegetables like broccoli florets, carrot sticks, and cauliflower florets are negligibly handled to lessen planning time. These items are normally found in the produce part of supermarkets.

Frozen Vegetables: Frozen vegetables, like peas, corn, and green beans, are much of the time negligibly handled through whitening and speedy freezing. This jam their supplement content and flavor for expanded time span of usability.

Dried Organic products: Dried organic products like raisins, apricots, and dates are gotten by eliminating the water content, saving the regular sugars and supplements. They make for helpful, rack stable bites.

Grains:

Earthy colored Rice: Earthy colored rice is a negligibly handled grain that holds its external wheat and microbe layers, making it plentiful in fiber, nutrients, and minerals. It is less refined than white rice.

Entire Wheat Bread: Entire wheat bread is produced using negligibly handled entire grains, keeping up with the wheat and microbe. It offers higher fiber and supplement content contrasted with white bread.

Steel-Cut Oats: Steel-cut oats are insignificantly handled, with just the external husk eliminated. They give a generous, nutty surface and are an incredible wellspring of dissolvable fiber.

Quinoa: Quinoa is an insignificantly handled pseudo-grain, valued for its high protein content and supplement thickness. It is consumed as entire seeds or utilized in different dishes.

Natural Corn: Fresh corn and dried corn parts are instances of insignificantly handled corn items. They are less refined than cornmeal and corn syrup.

Meats and Proteins:

New Fish Filet: A new fish filet, like salmon, cod, or tilapia, is an insignificantly handled protein source. It is commonly sold without added flavors or added substances.

Poultry: Unseasoned chicken bosoms and turkey cuts are instances of insignificantly handled poultry items. They are liberated from marinades and added substances.

Lean Hamburger: Lean cuts of meat, similar to sirloin or tenderloin, are negligibly handled meats that are low in fat and unseasoned.

Eggs: Eggs in their regular state are negligibly handled. They are a nutritious wellspring of protein, nutrients, and minerals.

Vegetables: Dried vegetables, like lentils, chickpeas, and dark beans, are insignificantly handled plant-based proteins. They can be doused and cooked for different dishes.

Dairy Items:
Natural Milk: New milk, whether from cows, goats, or different warm blooded creatures, is negligibly handled and can be drunk with no guarantees or utilized in the planning of dairy items.

Plain Yogurt: Plain yogurt is an insignificantly handled dairy item produced using milk and live bacterial societies. It is a wellspring of probiotics and protein.

Cheddar: Numerous assortments of cheddar, like cheddar, mozzarella, and Swiss, are viewed as insignificantly handled dairy items. They are made through the maturation of milk with insignificant added substances.

Margarine: Spread, particularly unsalted margarine, is an insignificantly handled dairy item produced using cream or milk, with few extra fixings.

Nuts and Seeds:
Crude Almonds: Crude almonds are insignificantly handled nuts that poor person been cooked or salted. They are wealthy in sound fats, protein, and fundamental supplements.

Regular Peanut Butter: Normal peanut butter is produced using negligibly handled peanuts, with no additional sugars or hydrogenated oils. It is an astounding wellspring of protein and solid fats.

Chia Seeds: Chia seeds are negligibly handled seeds that can be consumed overall, giving a rich wellspring of fiber, omega-3 unsaturated fats, and different supplements.

Hemp Seeds: Hemp seeds are insignificantly handled seeds with a nutty flavor and a wholesome profile that incorporates protein, sound fats, and fundamental amino acids.

Sunflower Seeds: Crude sunflower seeds are negligibly handled and are a wellspring of nutrients, minerals, and sound fats.

Spices and Flavors:
New Spices: Spices like basil, cilantro, and parsley are insignificantly handled flavors that add new flavor to dishes.

Entire Flavors: Entire flavors, for example, entire cinnamon sticks, entire cloves, and entire dark peppercorns, are negligibly handled and hold their regular fragrances and flavors.

Dried Spices: Dried spices like oregano, thyme, and rosemary are negligibly handled flavors that are helpful for long haul stockpiling.

Refreshments:
Water: Water is a definitive negligibly handled refreshment, giving fundamental hydration without added substances.

Newly Crushed Juice: Newly pressed leafy foods juices, produced using entire produce, are negligibly handled and hold their regular flavors and supplements.

Unflavored Tea: Unflavored teas, like dark, green, white, and home grown teas, are negligibly handled and give an assortment of medical advantages.

Espresso Beans: Espresso beans, in their entire, unroasted structure, are negligibly handled and are simmered prior to preparing.

Sugars:

Crude Honey: Crude honey is a negligibly handled regular sugar created by honey bees. It is known for its normal pleasantness and potential medical advantages.

Maple Syrup: Unadulterated maple syrup is an insignificantly handled sugar produced using the sap of sugar maple trees. It is a characteristic option in contrast to profoundly refined syrups.

These instances of negligibly handled food sources feature the variety and overflow of choices accessible to purchasers who look to embrace an eating regimen that focuses on new, entire, and pure fixings. The utilization of such food sources gives an establishment to a reasonable and wellbeing cognizant way to deal with eating while at the same time cultivating a more profound association with the wellsprings of our food and the rich flavors and supplements they offer.

Chapter 5

Sustainable Farming Practices

Supportable cultivating rehearses certainly stand out enough to be noticed as of late as the worldwide populace proceeds to develop, and the interest for food, fiber, and fuel increases. The customary strategies for horticulture, portrayed by weighty synthetic use, over the top water utilization, and soil corruption, are ending up impractical over the long haul. Because of these difficulties, ranchers, specialists, and policymakers are investigating and executing different maintainable cultivating practices to guarantee food security, safeguard the climate, and advance financial practicality.

One of the critical standards of practical cultivating is the safeguarding of regular assets. This includes rehearses that limit soil disintegration, decrease water utilization, and safeguard biodiversity. One such methodology is the reception of no-till or decreased till cultivating. Dissimilar to customary furrowing, these strategies leave crop deposits on the field after gather, which forestalls soil disintegration and further develops soil structure. Furthermore, decreased culturing practices can lessen fuel utilization and ozone depleting substance emanations from cultivating tasks, adding to a more economical horticulture area.

Crop revolution is one more basic part of maintainable cultivating. By substituting the sorts of yields filled in a field, ranchers can decrease the gamble of soil exhaustion and vermin. This training further develops soil wellbeing as well as keeps a decent environment, as various harvests draw in different useful bugs and microorganisms. Crop turn can likewise upgrade supplement cycling and decrease the requirement for manufactured manures, making it a practical and harmless to the ecosystem approach.

Manageable cultivating rehearses likewise center around decreasing the utilization of engineered synthetic substances in horticulture. Incorporated bug the board (IPM) is a technique that advances the insignificant utilization of pesticides while controlling irritations successfully. IPM joins natural, mechanical, and synthetic techniques to oversee bothers, stressing avoidance and checking. This approach decreases the ecological effect of cultivating as well as limits the gamble of pesticide opposition in bug populaces.

Natural cultivating is a notable manageable practice that disposes of the utilization of engineered pesticides and manures. Natural ranches depend on regular techniques, for example, fertilizing the soil, cover editing, and harvest revolution to keep up with soil ripeness and control bugs. Natural cultivating likewise focuses on the prosperity of domesticated animals by giving admittance to the outside and disallowing the utilization of development chemicals and anti-toxins. These practices bring about better food as well as lessen the ecological effect of farming by disposing of substance spillover and the arrival of ozone harming substances related with manufactured manures.

Supportable cultivating rehearses reach out past harvest creation to domesticated animals the board. Rotational brushing is a strategy that permits domesticated animals to brush on various fields in an arranged and controlled way. This approach forestalls overgrazing, decreases soil compaction, and keeps up with the strength of prairies. Furthermore, it can upgrade carbon sequestration in the dirt, moderating environmental change. Coordinating animals with crop cultivating in agroecosystems can make collaborations between the two, like involving creature excrement as compost, accordingly expanding asset proficiency.

Water the board is a critical worry in reasonable cultivating. Customary water system practices can prompt water squander, soil saltiness, and spring exhaustion. Trickle water system, then again, is a more proficient and economical strategy that conveys water straightforwardly to establish roots, limiting dissipation and water overflow. Water collecting and the utilization of downpour barrels are additionally successful methodologies for monitoring water assets, especially in districts with water shortage.

Agroforestry is a supportable cultivating practice that consolidates tree development with yield or animals creation. Trees give various advantages, like shade, windbreaks, and expanded biodiversity. The underground roots of trees additionally assist with forestalling soil disintegration and further develop soil structure. Agroforestry frameworks can sequester carbon and upgrade the general flexibility of rural biological systems.

Economical cultivating rehearses additionally advance the utilization of cover crops. These are non-reaped plants that are developed principally to safeguard and work on the dirt. Cover crops assist with forestalling disintegration, stifle weeds, and improve soil fruitfulness by adding natural matter. They can likewise break infection and vermin cycles by upsetting their life cycles. Leguminous cover crops, similar to clover and hay, have the additional advantage of fixing nitrogen from the air, lessening the requirement for manufactured composts.

The protection of hereditary variety is one more fundamental component of economical cultivating. Monoculture cultivating, which depends on a predetermined number of harvest assortments, can make rural frameworks powerless against infections and vermin. Keeping a different genetic supply of harvests and domesticated animals can help shield against such dangers. Seed banks and rearing projects are apparatuses that help hereditary variety in horticulture.

Supportable cultivating rehearses put areas of strength for an on soil wellbeing. Sound soils are overflowing with microorganisms, which work with supplement cycling and work on supplement accessibility to plants. Rehearses like treating the soil and the expansion of natural make a difference to the dirt can upgrade soil structure and microbial movement. Solid soils likewise have a higher water-holding limit, lessening the requirement for water system and improving dry spell flexibility.

Maintainable cultivating rehearses have shown extraordinary commitment in working on the ecological manageability of farming, yet they likewise have financial advantages. While the underlying progress to supportable cultivating might require interests in new hardware and practices, long haul reserve funds can be critical. Diminished pesticide and manure use, lower water utilization, and further developed soil wellbeing can all prompt expense reserve funds for ranchers. Moreover, the developing buyer interest for reasonably created food can prompt greater costs and market open doors for ranchers who embrace these practices.

Moreover, manageable cultivating can make nearby positions and animate provincial economies. Limited scope, broadened cultivating frameworks are many times more work serious than enormous scope monoculture activities. These frameworks require a more extensive scope of abilities and proposition open doors for work in different parts of farming. Furthermore, the advancement of nearby and natural food creation can prompt the improvement of neighborhood food showcases and expanded financial versatility in country networks.

Feasible cultivating rehearses likewise assume a vital part in tending to environmental change. Horticulture is both a wellspring of ozone harming substance emanations and an expected sink for carbon. Emanations from agribusiness fundamentally come from the utilization of engineered composts, the energy utilization of homestead apparatus, and the arrival of methane from animals. Manageable cultivating practices can altogether lessen these emanations. For instance, the utilization of natural cultivating strategies diminishes the energy and emanations related with engineered compost creation and application. Moreover, agroforestry and cover trimming can sequester carbon in soils and plant biomass, assisting with counterbalancing outflows from different sources.

Supportable cultivating practices can likewise add to environmental change variation. The rising recurrence of outrageous climate occasions, like dry seasons and floods, represents a critical danger to farming.

Reasonable practices like cover trimming and agroforestry can upgrade soil flexibility and water maintenance, making ranches stronger to these difficulties. Additionally, enhancing yields and utilizing privately adjusted assortments can assist agribusiness with adjusting to changing environment conditions.

Notwithstanding the ecological and monetary advantages, maintainable cultivating rehearses offer various social benefits. They focus on the prosperity of farmworkers by lessening their openness to destructive pesticides and encouraging more secure working circumstances. Besides, supportable farming frequently puts areas of strength for an on local area inclusion and participation. Ranchers who embrace economical practices might take part in neighborhood food organizations, local area upheld farming projects, and different drives that cultivate social associations and backing nearby economies.

Be that as it may, the reception of reasonable cultivating rehearses isn't without challenges. Changing from ordinary to reasonable techniques can be a complex and tedious cycle. It might require changes in cultivating methods, gear, and foundation, which can be expensive and problematic. Ranchers may likewise confront opposition from laid out industry standards and practices.

Admittance to data and training is one more hindrance to the broad reception of supportable cultivating rehearses. Numerous ranchers come up short on information and assets to arrive at informed conclusions about economical farming. Outreach programs, specialized help, and rancher to-rancher networks are fundamental for spreading data and working with the change to manageable cultivating.

Also, maintainable cultivating practices may not be reasonable for all rural frameworks and districts. Factors, for example, environment, soil type, and neighborhood economic situations can impact the plausibility of specific practices. Taking into account these variables and designer manageable cultivating ways to deal with nearby contexts is fundamental.

Feasible cultivating rehearses are frequently connected with more limited size, differentiated cultivating activities. While these techniques offer various advantages, they might confront difficulties connected with economies of scale and market access. Huge monoculture cultivates frequently benefit from economies of scale, permitting them to deliver food at lower costs. Limited scope economical ranches may battle to contend in cost driven markets.

5.1 Organic farming and its principles

Natural cultivating is a rural methodology that puts areas of strength for an on maintainability, ecological security, and the prosperity of both the land and individuals who work it. Dissimilar to customary cultivating, which frequently depends on manufactured synthetic compounds and hereditarily altered creatures, natural cultivating plans to limit the utilization of such sources of info and expand the utilization of regular and harmless to the ecosystem strategies to keep up with soil ripeness, control bugs, and advance harvest development.

The rules that underlie natural cultivating guide the practices and ways of thinking of the individuals who pick this way to deal with farming.

One of the essential standards of natural cultivating is soil wellbeing and fruitfulness. Natural ranchers perceive that dirt is the groundwork of a solid and useful homestead. They focus on the utilization of natural matter, for example, fertilizer, cover harvests, and green composts, to further develop soil structure, supplement content, and microbial action. By upgrading soil fruitfulness normally, natural cultivating plans to make a feasible starting point for horticultural efficiency that can be kept up with over the long haul.

Crop pivot is one more key standard of natural cultivating. Crop turn includes exchanging the kinds of yields filled in a specific field from one season to another. This training assists with breaking illness and irritation cycles, forestall soil exhaustion, and further develop soil wellbeing. Various yields have changing supplement needs and nuisance weaknesses, so by pivoting crops, natural ranchers can decrease the gamble of issues related with monoculture cultivating. Besides, crop turn upholds biodiversity in the horticultural environment, drawing in a different scope of helpful bugs and microorganisms.

Weed and bug the executives are fundamental parts of natural cultivating, and the standards directing these practices underscore avoidance and normal control techniques. Natural ranchers use coordinated bother the board (IPM) techniques, joining organic, mechanical, and substance strategies to oversee bugs really while limiting the utilization of engineered pesticides. This approach decreases the ecological effect of cultivating as well as forestalls the advancement of pesticide-safe vermin populaces. In natural cultivating, the accentuation is on making a decent environment where vermin are held under wraps by regular hunters.

The standard of biodiversity assumes a crucial part in natural cultivating. By differentiating the plant and animal species present in a rural framework, natural ranchers can improve environment flexibility. For instance, establishing hedgerows and giving territory to pollinators can further develop fertilization administrations for crops. Coordinating animals into crop cultivating frameworks can likewise make cooperative energies, with creature compost filling in as an important manure and cover crops giving search and disintegration control. The coordination of various components in a farming framework improves its general maintainability.

One more center rule of natural cultivating is the restriction of manufactured synthetic substances, including engineered composts and pesticides. Natural cultivating depends on regular other options and non-compound strategies to address the difficulties of bug control, weed administration, and soil ripeness. By keeping away from manufactured synthetic compounds, natural cultivating expects to lessen ecological pollution, limit damage to non-target species, and safeguard the wellbeing of farmworkers and purchasers. This obligation to synthetic free farming is a characterizing component of the natural methodology.

Hereditary change is one more practice that is precluded in natural cultivating. Natural norms commonly disallow the utilization of hereditarily adjusted living beings (GMOs) in crop creation and creature cultivation. The reasoning behind this preclusion is to safeguard the hereditary honesty of natural harvests and to guarantee the security and wellbeing of purchasers. Natural cultivating looks to keep up with regular hereditary variety and forestall accidental biological results related with GMOs.

Rather than traditional cultivating, which frequently depends on monoculture practices and huge scope motorization, natural cultivating advances variety in agrarian frameworks and stresses more limited size and work concentrated strategies. Limited scope, differentiated cultivating frameworks are many times stronger and harmless to the ecosystem, as they emulate regular environments and can diminish the requirement for compound information sources. By advancing variety in yields and animals, natural cultivating upholds neighborhood and local food frameworks and decreases the ecological effect of horticulture.

The standard of straightforwardness and recognizability is vital to natural cultivating. Natural affirmation and naming give customers data about the starting points and strategies used to deliver their food. Confirmation offices guarantee that natural homesteads stick to natural norms, permitting customers to pursue informed decisions about the items they buy. This straightforwardness fabricates trust as well as spurs a market interest for natural items.

Animal government assistance is a basic thought in natural cultivating, especially in animals tasks. Natural norms commonly expect that creatures approach the outside and that they are brought up in conditions that consider regular ways of behaving. The utilization of development chemicals and anti-infection agents is frequently precluded, adding to the prosperity of the creatures and lessening the gamble of anti-microbial obstruction. Natural domesticated animals cultivating plans to make conditions that are more in accordance with the creatures' regular ways of behaving and needs.

The rule of social obligation in natural cultivating envelops the prosperity of farmworkers and networks. Natural cultivating frequently depends on work escalated rehearses, and the accentuation on ecological stewardship reaches out to individuals who work on natural ranches. Fair work rehearses, safe working circumstances, and evenhanded remuneration are essential parts of natural cultivating. Furthermore, natural cultivating can add to the advancement of nearby economies and local area inclusion through the advancement of neighborhood and provincial food frameworks.

Natural cultivating standards focus on the utilization of sustainable assets and the decrease of waste. By limiting the utilization of manufactured inputs and advancing regular techniques for vermin and infectious prevention, natural cultivating moderates assets and diminishes the ecological effect of farming. Moreover, natural cultivating frequently incorporates practices, for example, fertilizing the soil and reusing, which assist with limiting waste and advance asset proficiency.

Natural cultivating is administered by unambiguous guidelines and guidelines that fluctuate by nation and district. These guidelines are intended with guarantee that natural practices comply to the center standards of natural cultivating. Accreditation offices are liable for checking that ranches and items satisfy these guidelines, and they lead investigations to survey consistence. Natural accreditation names furnish buyers with affirmation that the items they buy have been delivered as per natural standards and principles.

The improvement of natural cultivating guidelines has been basic to the development of the natural area and the foundation of buyer trust. These norms cover a large number of practices and prerequisites, from soil the executives and vermin control to creature government assistance and handling techniques. They likewise determine which data sources and substances are permitted and restricted in natural cultivating.

The standards of natural cultivating have been created over many years and are ceaselessly advancing to address new difficulties and potential open doors in agribusiness. As purchaser interest for natural items has developed, so too has the requirement for clear and steady guidelines. The improvement of global natural principles, like those laid out by the Global League of Natural Horticulture Developments (IFOAM), has made a typical system for natural cultivating rehearses around the world.

Natural cultivating isn't without its difficulties. Pundits contend that natural cultivating may not be essentially as useful as ordinary cultivating, prompting worries about food security and moderateness. Natural ranches frequently yield somewhat less per section of land in contrast with ordinary homesteads, essentially because of limitations on engineered manures and pesticides. Nonetheless, advocates of natural cultivating contend that this distinction can be counterbalanced by further developed soil wellbeing and lower input costs. They likewise underscore that natural cultivating puts serious areas of strength for an on long haul supportability and environment wellbeing.

Market access is one more test for natural ranchers. While the interest for natural items is developing, some enormous scope ware markets are intended for mass deals, making it challenging for little and medium-sized natural ranchers to get to these business sectors. Natural ranchers might have to investigate elective showcasing channels, for example, ranchers' business sectors, local area upheld horticulture projects, and neighborhood food organizations, to arrive at purchasers ready to pay a premium for natural food.

Natural cultivating practices can likewise confront analysis connected with the affirmation and administrative interaction. Some contend that natural principles might change starting with one locale then onto the next, prompting irregularities in what is thought of "natural." There can likewise be difficulties in implementing and confirming consistence with natural guidelines, especially in instances of deceitful marking or distortion.

5.2 Regenerative agriculture and soil health

Regenerative horticulture is a creative and all encompassing way to deal with cultivating that focuses on soil wellbeing as the underpinning of a versatile and maintainable food framework. This rural way of thinking looks to reestablish and upgrade the soundness of soils, at last prompting further developed crop efficiency, decreased ecological effect, and the alleviation of environmental change. Regenerative horticulture envelops a scope of practices and rules that work as one to revive and support the dirt, making it a useful asset for tending to a large number of the squeezing difficulties confronting present day farming.

One of the central standards of regenerative agribusiness is the emphasis on soil wellbeing. Sound soil is the backbone of any ranch, and regenerative practices expect to reestablish and keep up with soil imperativeness. This involves encouraging the improvement of a strong soil structure, working on supplement content, and advancing a flourishing soil microbiome. By making conditions that help soil wellbeing, regenerative farming upgrades its ability to give fundamental biological system administrations, like water filtration, supplement cycling, and carbon sequestration.

Regenerative horticulture standards frequently include lessening or disposing of soil unsettling influence. Dissimilar to regular cultivating rehearses that depend on culturing, regenerative methodologies, for example, no-till or diminished till cultivating, focus on negligible soil aggravation. These practices keep up with the trustworthiness of the dirt design, forestall disintegration, and safeguard gainful soil microorganisms, which are basic for supplement cycling and by and large soil wellbeing. Lessening soil aggravation can likewise assist with limiting the arrival of put away carbon into the climate, adding to carbon sequestration.

The mix of cover crops is one more focal component of regenerative agribusiness. Cover crops are non-reaped plants developed fundamentally to safeguard and work on the dirt. They assume a critical part in forestalling disintegration, smothering weeds, and upgrading soil richness by adding natural matter. Cover crops likewise assist with breaking sickness and nuisance cycles by upsetting their life cycles. By cultivating biodiversity and adding natural make a difference to the dirt, cover crops are a critical part in reestablishing and keeping up with soil wellbeing.

Broadening yield and animals frameworks is an essential guideline of regenerative farming. Monoculture cultivating, which depends on the broad development of a solitary harvest, can drain soil supplements and advance vermin and sickness pressures. Regenerative practices, then again, energize crop turns and the development of various harvests. This variety assists upgrade with ruining wellbeing, diminish the requirement for manufactured manures, and draw in a more extensive scope of useful bugs and microorganisms.

The standards of regenerative agribusiness additionally underline diminishing the dependence on engineered synthetics. While regular horticulture frequently relies upon manufactured pesticides and composts, regenerative methodologies try to limit their utilization.

All things considered, they advance the utilization of normal other options, like fertilizer, mulch, and valuable bugs, to oversee bothers and further develop soil fruitfulness. This change away from engineered synthetics safeguards the climate, decrease the gamble of pesticide opposition in bother populaces, and backing soil wellbeing.

Regenerative agribusiness additionally perceives the significance of coordinating domesticated animals into cultivating frameworks. The presence of creatures can improve supplement cycling and natural matter decay. Rehearses like rotational touching, in which animals brush on various fields in an arranged and controlled way, forestall overgrazing and advance soil wellbeing. The reconciliation of animals into regenerative cultivating frameworks makes cooperative energies, with creature compost filling in as an important manure and cover crops giving search and disintegration control.

Effective water the executives is one more key standard of regenerative farming. Ordinary water system practices can prompt water squander, soil saltiness, and spring exhaustion. Regenerative practices, for example, trickle water system, intend to utilize water all the more productively by conveying it straightforwardly to establish roots, limiting dissipation and spillover. Water collecting and the utilization of downpour barrels are additionally successful methodologies for preserving water assets, especially in locales with water shortage.

Agroforestry is a regenerative methodology that consolidates tree development with yield or animals creation. Trees give various advantages, like shade, windbreaks, and expanded biodiversity. The root foundations of trees assist with forestalling soil disintegration and further develop soil structure, while agroforestry frameworks can sequester carbon and improve the general strength of rural biological systems. Agroforestry advances soil wellbeing as well as adds to environmental change moderation.

Regenerative farming puts major areas of strength for an on the preservation of hereditary variety. Keeping a different genetic supply of yields and domesticated animals can help protect against infections, bugs, and changing natural circumstances. Seed banks and reproducing programs are apparatuses that help hereditary variety in horticulture and guarantee the flexibility of food creation frameworks.

Notwithstanding the ecological advantages, regenerative agribusiness offers various financial benefits. While the underlying progress to regenerative practices might require interests in new gear and practices, long haul reserve funds can be huge. Decreased pesticide and compost use, lower water utilization, and further developed soil wellbeing can all prompt expense reserve funds for ranchers. Moreover, the developing interest for economically created food can bring about greater costs and market open doors for ranchers who embrace regenerative practices.

The reception of regenerative horticulture can likewise make neighborhood occupations and animate provincial economies. Limited scope, enhanced cultivating frameworks are much of the time more work escalated than enormous scope monoculture activities.

These frameworks require a more extensive scope of abilities and proposition valuable open doors for work in different parts of horticulture. Also, the advancement of nearby and feasible food creation can prompt the improvement of neighborhood food advertises and expanded financial versatility in rustic networks.

Regenerative horticulture assumes a significant part in tending to environmental change. Farming is both a wellspring of ozone harming substance emanations and a possible sink for carbon. Outflows from horticulture essentially come from the utilization of manufactured manures, the energy utilization of ranch apparatus, and the arrival of methane from animals. Regenerative practices can essentially decrease these discharges. For instance, the utilization of natural cultivating strategies decreases the energy and outflows related with manufactured manure creation and application. Besides, agroforestry and cover trimming can sequester carbon in soils and plant biomass, assisting with counterbalancing discharges from different sources.

Regenerative horticulture likewise adds to environmental change variation. The rising recurrence of outrageous climate occasions, like dry spells and floods, represents a critical danger to farming. Regenerative practices like cover trimming and agroforestry improve soil versatility and water maintenance, making ranches stronger to these difficulties. Furthermore, differentiating yields and utilizing privately adjusted assortments can assist agribusiness with adjusting to changing environment conditions.

Notwithstanding the natural, financial, and environment benefits, regenerative farming offers social benefits. It focuses on the prosperity of farmworkers by lessening their openness to unsafe pesticides and cultivating more secure working circumstances. Moreover, regenerative horticulture frequently puts major areas of strength for an on local area inclusion and participation. Ranchers who embrace regenerative practices might participate in neighborhood food organizations, local area upheld horticulture programs, and different drives that encourage social associations and backing nearby economies.

The reception of regenerative agribusiness isn't without challenges. Progressing from regular to regenerative strategies can be a complex and tedious interaction. It might require changes in cultivating methods, hardware, and foundation, which can be exorbitant and troublesome. Ranchers may likewise confront opposition from laid out industry standards and practices.

Admittance to data and schooling is one more obstruction to the boundless reception of regenerative horticulture. Numerous ranchers come up short on information and assets to settle on informed conclusions about regenerative practices. Outreach programs, specialized help, and rancher to-rancher networks are fundamental for dispersing data and working with the change to regenerative cultivating.

Strategy support is basic to conquering these difficulties and advancing regenerative horticulture. State run administrations and global associations can give motivations and monetary help to empower the reception of regenerative practices. Appropriations, charge motivations, and specialized help can assist with counterbalancing the underlying expenses of changing to regenerative cultivating. Guideline and confirmation frameworks can likewise assume a part in advancing regenerative horticulture by furnishing customers with data about the supportability of the items they buy.

5.3 Reducing synthetic chemicals and pesticides

The decrease of engineered synthetic compounds and pesticides in farming is a basic part of endeavors to make a more practical and harmless to the ecosystem food framework. Engineered synthetic compounds and pesticides have been broadly utilized in ordinary farming to battle bothers, control illnesses, and improve crop yields. Notwithstanding, the exorbitant utilization of these synthetic compounds affects the climate, human wellbeing, and the improvement of pesticide-safe irritations. Subsequently, there is a developing development to lessen the dependence on engineered synthetic substances and pesticides in horticulture and investigate elective, more economical methodologies.

One of the really main thrusts behind the decrease of engineered synthetic substances and pesticides is the worry about their ecological effect. Substance pesticides can taint soil and water, hurt non-target species, and disturb environments. Spillover from fields treated with pesticides can stream into adjacent water bodies, making water contamination and mischief oceanic life. The gathering of manufactured synthetics in the climate can have sweeping ramifications for biological systems and biodiversity.

Furthermore, the utilization of manufactured synthetic compounds in horticulture adds to ozone depleting substance discharges. The creation and use of engineered manures, pesticides, and herbicides require critical energy input and can bring about outflows of carbon dioxide (CO_2) and other ozone depleting substances. Besides, the breakdown of specific manufactured synthetics in the dirt can deliver nitrous oxide (N_2O), a powerful ozone depleting substance. Diminishing the utilization of these synthetic compounds can assist with moderating the rural area's commitment to environmental change.

Human wellbeing concerns likewise assume an essential part in the push to decrease engineered substance and pesticide use in horticulture. Openness to pesticide build-ups on food, in drinking water, or in the air can have antagonistic wellbeing impacts, going from intense harming to constant medical conditions. Pesticide deposits have been connected to different medical problems, including disease, neurological issues, and regenerative issues. Safeguarding the strength of farmworkers, close by networks, and customers is a huge driver for tracking down options in contrast to engineered synthetics and pesticides.

Besides, the improvement of pesticide-safe irritations has turned into a critical issue in current farming. The weighty and ceaseless utilization of synthetic pesticides can prompt the development of irritations that are impervious to these synthetic substances. This obstruction decreases the viability of compound pesticides as well as requires the advancement of additional strong and earth harming details. Subsequently, the pattern of pesticide opposition keeps, intensifying the requirement for progressively harmful synthetics.

To address these worries and decrease the dependence on manufactured synthetic compounds and pesticides, a few systems and approaches have been created and carried out:

Incorporated Vermin The executives (IPM): IPM is a complete methodology that consolidates different systems to oversee bugs really while limiting the utilization of manufactured pesticides. IPM methodologies incorporate natural control, social practices, crop revolution, and the utilization of vermin safe harvest assortments. Checking and avoidance are additionally key parts of IPM, permitting ranchers to distinguish and address bother issues before they become serious. By lessening the dependence on engineered synthetic compounds, IPM advances supportable and harmless to the ecosystem bug the executives.

Natural Cultivating: Natural cultivating is a creation framework that evades the utilization of engineered pesticides and substance manures. All things considered, natural ranchers depend on normal other options, for example, helpful bugs, cover yields, and manure, to oversee irritations and upgrade soil fruitfulness. Natural practices focus on the prosperity of the climate, farmworkers, and customers by restricting the utilization of manufactured synthetics and advancing manageable horticulture.

Agroecological Cultivating: Agroecology is a way to deal with cultivating that accentuates the reconciliation of natural standards into agrarian practices. It centers around making different and tough cultivating frameworks that are less dependent on manufactured synthetics. Agroecological cultivating advances the utilization of practices like intercropping, polyculture, and crop revolution to upgrade regular nuisance control and decrease the requirement for synthetic pesticides.

Organic Control: Organic control includes the utilization of normal hunters, parasites, and microbes to oversee bug populaces. This approach bridles the force of the environment to manage bug numbers and diminish the requirement for engineered pesticides. Instances of natural control incorporate delivering ladybugs to control aphids or utilizing nematodes to target soil-staying nuisances.

Plant Rearing: Creating crop assortments that are impervious to irritations and sicknesses is one more system to decrease the requirement for engineered pesticides. This can be accomplished through conventional rearing techniques or, at times, hereditary change. Safe harvest assortments are a proactive way to deal with bug the executives, as they decrease weakness to bug harm.

Trap Harvests: Trap crops are plants that are purposefully planted to draw in bothers from the principal crop. By focusing nuisances on unambiguous plants, ranchers can decrease harm to the essential yield and breaking point the requirement for substance pesticides. Trap editing is a powerful, harmless to the ecosystem strategy for bother control.

Helpful Bugs: Numerous bugs act as normal hunters of rural nuisances. Empowering the presence of valuable bugs, like ladybugs, parasitic wasps, and lacewings, can assist with controlling nuisance populaces. Ranches can give natural surroundings and food sources to these bugs to help their populaces and lessen the dependence on synthetic pesticides.

Non-Compound Medicines: Non-substance medicines, like heated water, steam, and bright light, can be utilized to oversee bothers without the utilization of engineered pesticides. These strategies are progressively being investigated as choices for bug control.

Checking and Early Discovery: Ordinary observing of irritation populaces and early recognition of bug pervasions are basic parts of nuisance the board. By recognizing and tending to bug issues early, ranchers can frequently forestall the requirement for synthetic pesticides.

Rotational and Broadened Cultivating: Yield turn and expansion of cultivating frameworks can assist with breaking nuisance cycles and lessen the development of irritations in a given region. These practices upgrade the general flexibility of farming and breaking point the dependence on manufactured synthetic substances.

Schooling and Expansion Administrations: Furnishing ranchers with training and specialized help on elective irritation the board rehearses is fundamental for effective reception. Expansion administrations and preparing projects can assist ranchers with changing away from manufactured pesticides and take on additional reasonable practices.

Administrative Measures: States and administrative organizations assume a fundamental part in diminishing the utilization of manufactured synthetic substances and pesticides in farming. They can lay out and implement limitations on the utilization of specific synthetic compounds and advance the reception of elective practices through approaches, motivators, and guidelines.

It is fundamental to recognize that the progress away from engineered synthetic substances and pesticides in farming may not be without challenges. Ranchers frequently face the requirement for schooling, specialized help, and admittance to assets to effectively take on elective practices. Now and again, there might be monetary requirements related with the shift to more supportable vermin the board techniques. In any case, the drawn out advantages of diminished substance dependence, worked on ecological manageability, and the assurance of human wellbeing make these difficulties advantageous.

The reception of elective irritation the executives rehearses and the decrease of manufactured synthetics and pesticides in farming are fundamental stages towards making a more manageable and harmless to the ecosystem food framework. These methodologies not just safeguard the climate, defend human wellbeing, and lessen ozone depleting substance discharges yet in addition add to stronger and monetarily suitable rural frameworks. As the worldwide local area keeps on wrestling with the results of modern horticulture, the reception of these practices offers a promising way ahead in tending to the squeezing difficulties within recent memory.

Chapter 6

Food Safety and Traceability

Sanitation and recognizability are two pivotal parts of the cutting edge food industry. They assume a significant part in guaranteeing that the food we devour is protected, dependable, and of superior grade. In this 1900-word exposition, we will investigate the meaning of food handling and recognizability, the difficulties they present, and the mechanical progressions that have been made to resolve these issues.

Food handling is principal in the food business, as it straightforwardly influences the wellbeing and prosperity of customers. Debased or dangerous food can prompt foodborne sicknesses, which can be serious and, surprisingly, deadly. Subsequently, guaranteeing the security of food items is an essential worry for food makers, administrative specialists, and purchasers the same.

One of the essential goals of sanitation is to forestall foodborne sicknesses by carrying out rigid cleanliness and quality control estimates all through the food production network. These actions incorporate the review of natural substances, the observing of creation processes, and the testing of end results for toxins like microorganisms, synthetic compounds, and allergens. Also, legitimate capacity and transportation rehearses are fundamental to keeping up with the wellbeing and nature of food items.

Discernibility, then again, alludes to the capacity to follow the development of food items through the store network from the starting place to the purchaser. This is critical because of multiple factors. It, first and foremost, takes into consideration the speedy ID and review of possibly tainted or risky items. In case of a food handling issue, discernibility frameworks can pinpoint the wellspring of the issue and empower the expulsion of impacted items from the market, forestalling further damage to purchasers.

Also, detectability upgrades straightforwardness in the food store network. Purchasers are progressively keen on knowing where their food comes from, the way things were delivered, and whether it meets specific moral and ecological norms. Discernibility frameworks give this data, assisting purchasers with settling on informed decisions and considering food makers responsible for their practices.

In any case, accomplishing extensive food handling and discernibility isn't without its difficulties. The food store network is perplexing and frequently worldwide in scope, with items going through various stages and changing hands often previously arriving at the buyer. This intricacy can make it challenging to successfully screen and control the security and detectability of food items.

Moreover, the food business should fight with advancing dangers and dangers. New microorganisms and foreign substances can arise, and changing customer inclinations and worldwide guidelines can entangle the administration of sanitation and detectability. These difficulties highlight the requirement for creative arrangements and innovative headways.

One of the vital mechanical headways in the field of food handling and detectability is the reception of computerized frameworks and information examination. These advancements have altered the manner in which food makers and administrative specialists oversee and screen sanitation and detectability.

Advanced frameworks, for example, electronic record-keeping and information the executives, empower food makers to follow the creation, stockpiling, and transportation of their items all the more really. These frameworks not just work on the precision and effectiveness of record-keeping yet additionally empower continuous information sharing and correspondence across the inventory network. This considers quick reaction to sanitation episodes and convenient limited, the effect on purchasers.

Moreover, information examination assume a crucial part in evaluating and relieving sanitation chances. By investigating enormous volumes of information, for example, temperature and stickiness records, creation logs, and assessment results, it is feasible to distinguish possible issues before they heighten. Prescient examination, for example, can figure food handling gambles with in light of authentic information and patterns, assisting food makers with going to proactive lengths to forestall defilement and keep up with the wellbeing of their items.

Blockchain innovation has arisen as a distinct advantage in upgrading recognizability inside the food production network. Blockchain is a decentralized and secure computerized record that records exchanges in a straightforward and carefully designed way. When applied to the food business, blockchain can make a whole chain of data about the beginning, creation, and conveyance of food items.

Every member in the production network, from the rancher to the retailer, can record and confirm their exercises on the blockchain. This guarantees that the information stays exact and unaltered, giving a dependable wellspring of data for buyers and administrative specialists. In case of a sanitation issue, the blockchain can be utilized to follow back the impacted item to its source in no time, essentially diminishing the time and assets expected for reviews.

Blockchain innovation additionally addresses the rising purchaser interest for straightforwardness in the food production network. By checking a QR code or utilizing a cell phone application, customers can get to point by point data about the food item they are buying, including its starting point, creation techniques, and quality confirmations. This degree of straightforwardness assembles trust and permits purchasers to settle on informed decisions about the food they eat.

Be that as it may, the reception of these advances isn't without challenges. Carrying out computerized frameworks and blockchain innovation can be exorbitant and require massive changes to existing cycles. Furthermore, there is a requirement for vast guidelines and guidelines to guarantee interoperability and information consistency across the production network. These provokes should be addressed to understand the capability of these innovative progressions completely.

Notwithstanding advanced frameworks and blockchain, different innovations are likewise transforming the domain of sanitation and recognizability. For example, the Web of Things (IoT) is being utilized to screen and control different parts of food creation and conveyance. Sensors can follow temperature, dampness, and other ecological elements, giving constant information that guarantees the quality and security of food items. IoT gadgets can likewise be utilized to screen the state of vehicles utilized in food transportation, guaranteeing that temperature-delicate items stay inside safe cutoff points during travel.

Moreover, man-made reasoning (artificial intelligence) is being utilized to improve the speed and precision of food handling examinations. Man-made intelligence fueled picture acknowledgment frameworks can rapidly distinguish pollutants or abnormalities in food items, lessening the dependence on manual examination and human mistake. AI calculations can dissect tremendous measures of information to recognize examples and peculiarities, making it simpler to distinguish possible dangers and make restorative moves.

Mechanical mechanization is one more innovative headway that is building up some momentum in the food business. Robots can be utilized in different phases of creation, from reaping and handling to bundling and quality control. They can work in conditions that might be risky to people and perform redundant errands with accuracy and effectiveness. This further develops food handling as well as lessens work expenses and improves the consistency of food items.

Hereditary advances have likewise made critical commitments to sanitation and recognizability. DNA-based strategies are utilized to distinguish and follow the beginning of food items. DNA barcoding, for instance, considers the exact distinguishing proof of species in complex food items, which is essential for both sanitation and forestalling fake naming.

Nanotechnology is one more area of exploration that holds guarantee for further developing sanitation. Nanosensors can distinguish pollutants and microbes at the nanoscale, giving high responsiveness and particularity. This can prompt quicker and more precise testing techniques, diminishing the gamble of sullied items arriving at shoppers.

While these mechanical progressions offer huge potential in upgrading sanitation and recognizability, they likewise bring up significant moral and administrative issues. For example, the utilization of computer based intelligence in food handling examinations might prompt work dislodging for human auditors. Security concerns might emerge while gathering and sharing information in a blockchain-based framework. Besides, the likely abuse of hereditary and nanotechnology could present dangers, and administrative oversight is fundamental to guarantee the protected and mindful utilization of these advances.

6.1 Ensuring food safety in the Farm to Fork model

Guaranteeing sanitation in the Homestead to Fork model is a complex test that requires facilitated endeavors across the whole food production network. The Ranch to Fork model, otherwise called the food production network, envelops every one of the stages engaged with creating, handling, shipping, and conveying food to buyers. Guaranteeing the security of food at each step of this excursion is fundamental to safeguard general wellbeing and keep up with shopper certainty.

Food handling starts at the source, with the development of unrefined substances on ranches. Ranchers assume a basic part in guaranteeing that the food they produce is ok for utilization. This includes practices, for example, soil and water the board, bug control, and creature cultivation. These practices are fundamental for forestalling pollution of crude agrarian items with microorganisms, pesticides, and different impurities that can present dangers to human wellbeing.

Horticultural practices that focus on food handling incorporate the legitimate treatment of excrement, the utilization of safe water system water, and the use of fitting cleanliness measures while taking care of products of the soil. The utilization of pesticides and composts should likewise be painstakingly figured out how to keep compound buildups from surpassing safe cutoff points.

Besides, guaranteeing the security of creature inferred items like meat, eggs, and dairy starts with the wellbeing and government assistance of the actual creatures. Legitimate lodging, nourishment, and illness the executives are key parts in forestalling the transmission of microorganisms to these items. Ordinary reviews and veterinary consideration are significant for distinguishing and moderating any dangers.

The utilization of anti-infection agents in animal cultivating is an especially significant part of food handling. The abuse of anti-infection agents in animals can prompt the improvement of anti-toxin safe microorganisms, which can represent a critical general wellbeing danger. Guidelines and best practices have been laid out to restrict the utilization of anti-toxins in farming and to guarantee that any anti-infection agents utilized are controlled dependably and under veterinary watch.

Notwithstanding capable horticultural practices, one more basic part of guaranteeing food handling in the Homestead to Fork model is the legitimate dealing with and handling of unrefined components. In the wake of collecting, crude horticultural items frequently go through different handling steps, like washing, cutting, and bundling, before they arrive at customers. These cycles should be done under severe cleanliness conditions to forestall pollution.

Appropriate sterilization and cleanliness estimates in food handling offices are fundamental for forestalling the development of hurtful microorganisms and the advancement of foodborne microbes. This incorporates customary cleaning and sterilization of hardware and surfaces, as well as guaranteeing that representatives follow great assembling rehearses (GMPs) and stick to food handling conventions. Checking and confirmation processes, including microbiological testing, help to guarantee that food handling offices satisfy laid out security guidelines.

One more key worry in food handling is the gamble of cross-defilement. Cross-tainting happens when microbes starting with one food item are moved then onto the next. It can occur through shared gear, utensils, or surfaces. Forestalling cross-pollution is fundamental in offices where allergenic food sources are handled, as even little hints of allergens can set off serious unfavorably susceptible responses in delicate people.

To address the gamble of cross-defilement, food handling offices frequently carry out severe conventions, for example, variety coding for hardware and utensils to forestall misunderstandings, as well as isolating allergenic and non-allergenic food varieties to limit the gamble of incidental cross-contact. Representatives get preparing to guarantee they comprehend and follow these conventions reliably.

The transportation of food items is one more basic connection in the Ranch to Fork model, and it presents exceptional difficulties for food handling. During transportation, food items can be presented to temperature varieties, stickiness, and possible defilement from the climate or the actual vehicle. These elements can think twice about security and nature of the items being moved.

Refrigeration and temperature control are foremost during the transportation of transient food varieties, like meat, fish, and dairy items. Keeping up with appropriate temperature conditions is fundamental to forestall the development of microbes and the deterioration of food. Refrigerated trucks and temperature-checking frameworks are regularly used to guarantee that items stay inside the protected temperature range all through their excursion.

Notwithstanding temperature control, appropriate bundling and marking are urgent for sanitation during transportation. Bundling ought to be intended to shield food from actual harm and defilement. Names ought to give precise data about the item's starting point, taking care of directions, and any allergens or potential dangers related with the food.

Besides, the capacity and treatment of food items in retail foundations are key components in guaranteeing sanitation. Retailers are answerable for putting away food items at proper temperatures, keeping up with spotless and sterile conditions, and following safe food taking care of practices. This incorporates normal assessments of refrigeration units, legitimate revolution of transient items, and preparing for representatives on safe food taking care of.

Buyer schooling likewise assumes a crucial part in guaranteeing sanitation in the Ranch to Fork model. Buyers should know about legitimate food dealing with rehearses at home to lessen the gamble of foodborne sicknesses. This remembers rules for refrigeration, cooking temperatures, and the protected stockpiling of extras. Bringing issues to light about the significance of perusing food names to distinguish allergens and adhering to a particular taking care of directions is fundamental for forestalling unfriendly responses.

Administrative specialists at the neighborhood, public, and global levels have laid out norms and rules to guarantee food handling inside the Ranch to Fork model. These guidelines cover different parts of food creation, handling, and dissemination and are intended to safeguard general wellbeing and guarantee the nature of food items.

The reception and authorization of sanitation guidelines are fundamental to keeping up with exclusive requirements in the food business. Administrative organizations lead assessments and reviews of food foundations to guarantee consistence with these guidelines. Resistance can bring about punishments, reviews, or even lawful activity.

One of the most notable sanitation guidelines is the Risk Investigation and Basic Control Focuses (HACCP) framework. HACCP is an efficient way to deal with distinguishing and overseeing sanitation gambles. It includes evaluating the whole presentation process, recognizing basic control places where dangers can be controlled, and executing measures to forestall, dispose of, or decrease these dangers.

Sanitation guidelines are persistently refreshed and adjusted to answer arising dangers and difficulties. For instance, the expanded globalization of the food store network has prompted the improvement of worldwide principles, for example, those laid out by the Codex Alimentarius Commission, which sets rules for sanitation and quality around the world.

Lately, sanitation has turned into a more perplexing issue because of variables, for example, environmental change, arising microorganisms, and food extortion. Environmental change can influence the wellbeing of food by influencing the commonness and conveyance of microorganisms, modifying rural practices, and affecting foodborne illness designs.

In this manner, the food business should adjust to these changing circumstances by carrying out systems to moderate environment related gambles.

Arising microorganisms, like novel types of microbes or infections, represent a continuous danger to sanitation. These microorganisms might not have been recently experienced in the food production network, and their way of behaving and influence on human wellbeing can be eccentric. Fast recognition, checking, and research are critical to understanding and relieving the dangers presented by arising microorganisms.

Food extortion is one more worry in the Homestead to Fork model. Food misrepresentation happens when food items are intentionally mislabeled, subbed, or contaminated for monetary benefit. This can think twice about wellbeing and validness of food items. Normal types of food misrepresentation incorporate the mislabeling of items, weakening of fixings, and the utilization of mediocre or fake fixings.

To battle food extortion, innovation has turned into a significant apparatus. For example, DNA testing and fingerprinting strategies can confirm the credibility of food items by distinguishing the hereditary material of the fixings. Also, blockchain innovation can be utilized to make straightforward stock chains, making it more hard for deceitful practices to go undetected.

Notwithstanding the different difficulties and dangers in the Homestead to Fork model, it is fundamental to stress that the food business has made huge headways in guaranteeing food handling. These progressions have been driven by a mix of mechanical development, logical examination, administrative oversight, and a promise to further developing practices all through the store network.

6.2 Technology and traceability solutions

Innovation and discernibility arrangements have become fundamental devices in the present complex and globalized supply chains, empowering organizations to follow the development of items from their source to purchasers. These developments assume a vital part in further developing straightforwardness, quality, and wellbeing all through different businesses, from food to drugs. In this exposition, we will investigate the significance of innovation in detectability, the various arrangements accessible, and the expected advantages and difficulties related with their execution.

Innovation has reformed production network the executives by giving constant information and bits of knowledge that improve effectiveness, security, and responsibility. Recognizability, in this unique situation, alludes to the capacity to follow the progression of products and data inside the store network. It envelops different cycles, like checking, recording, and confirming the development of items, unrefined substances, and data. Innovation fills in as the empowering agent for productive and powerful recognizability arrangements, offering a variety of apparatuses and strategies to address the intricacies of present day supply chains.

One of the major advancements supporting detectability arrangements is the utilization of scanner tags and radio-recurrence ID (RFID) labels. Standardized identifications have been generally embraced for quite a long time and are found on practically all purchaser items. They contain data that can be immediately checked, taking into account prompt ID and following of the item. RFID labels, then again, utilize radio waves to communicate information to a peruser. They are further developed than scanner tags as they don't need direct view filtering and can store more data, making them valuable in different enterprises, including coordinated operations, medical care, and assembling.

Notwithstanding scanner tags and RFID, GPS (Worldwide Situating Framework) innovation is basic to discernibility in transportation and coordinated factors. GPS empowers exact area following, permitting organizations to screen the development of products progressively. This data enhances steering, diminish travel times, and work on the precision of conveyance assessments, which can be fundamental in time-delicate businesses.

Blockchain innovation, a decentralized and carefully designed computerized record, is arising as a strong answer for discernibility and straightforwardness. It makes a straightforward record of exchanges and occasions in a production network, guaranteeing that information can't be modified or erased. Every member in the production network can record and confirm their exercises on the blockchain, making a protected, changeless chain of data. This degree of straightforwardness is urgent in enterprises where responsibility, credibility, and discernibility are foremost, like food and drugs.

Blockchain innovation is especially valuable for guaranteeing the validness of items. Fake items are a critical concern, particularly in the drug business, where counterfeit meds can life-compromise. By executing blockchain-based recognizability, it turns out to be incredibly trying for fake items to penetrate the inventory network, as the whole history of an item's process is accessible for confirmation.

Besides, blockchain upgrades store network perceivability, making it simpler to quickly distinguish and redress issues. On account of an item review, blockchain empowers organizations to rapidly pinpoint the impacted things and the specific wellspring of defilement, forestalling further dispersion and expected mischief to customers.

In the food business, recognizability has turned into a critical component in guaranteeing wellbeing, quality, and straightforwardness. Foodborne diseases and defilement embarrassments have featured the significance of having the option to follow items back to their starting point. Different advancements, including barcoding, RFID, and blockchain, have been utilized to improve discernibility in the food store network.

Barcoding is regularly utilized in the food business to distinguish and follow items, from natural substances to completed products. It considers effective stock administration and improves on the following of items as they travel through the inventory network.

When joined with information the board frameworks, barcoding gives an exhaustive perspective on the store network, making it more straightforward to distinguish issues and keep up with the trustworthiness of the food items.

RFID labels are one more innovation utilized in the food business for detectability. They offer the upside of ongoing following and can be especially helpful for temperature-delicate items, guaranteeing that short-lived things are kept up with at the legitimate circumstances all through their excursion. RFID labels can likewise aid quality control by observing different boundaries, like temperature, dampness, and time span of usability, and giving bits of knowledge into the newness of items.

Blockchain innovation has made critical advances in the food business, principally because of its capacity to give straightforwardness and discernibility. It tends to worries connected with the beginning of food items, moral obtaining, and consistence with quality principles. With blockchain, customers can get to data about the whole excursion of a food item, including its source, creation strategies, certificates, and, surprisingly, the ranchers or makers included. This degree of straightforwardness assembles trust and permits buyers to go with informed decisions about the food they buy.

Besides, blockchain innovation can quickly distinguish and address food handling issues. In case of a tainting episode, the source can be pinpointed in no time, empowering proficient reviews and limiting mischief to customers. This diminishes the monetary and reputational harm that food organizations can endure during a review.

The drug business additionally intensely depends on innovation and detectability answers for guarantee the realness and security of items. Fake medications are a huge concern, and the results of phony prescriptions can be extreme. The utilization of blockchain in drugs can successfully battle duplicating, as it gives a protected and unchangeable record of each medication's excursion through the store network.

Serialization is one more innovation arrangement utilized in the drug business. It includes doling out an interesting chronic number to every unit of medicine, making it conceivable to follow the item at the singular level. This degree of granularity considers exact following and observing of every unit, assisting with guaranteeing the credibility and security of drugs.

With regards to drugs, RFID innovation is utilized to follow the development and capacity states of medications. RFID labels can be put on individual medication bundles or on beds and compartments, giving continuous information on their area and natural circumstances. This is especially significant for drugs that require explicit capacity conditions to keep up with their viability and wellbeing.

For discernibility in drugs, state run administrations and administrative organizations have carried out severe necessities. For instance, the Medication Store network Security Act (DSCSA) in the US orders the serialization of medication bundles and the foundation of an item following framework to get the drug inventory network. This is finished to forestall the presentation of fake or inadequate medications and to safeguard general wellbeing.

Mechanical progressions have likewise upgraded discernibility in the assembling business. Fabricating processes include the get together of different parts, frequently obtained from various providers. The capacity to follow these parts back to their source is fundamental for quality control and imperfection the executives.

Barcoding and RFID innovation are generally utilized in assembling to distinguish and follow parts. They empower makers to screen the creation cycle, identify deformities or inconsistencies, and follow back to the wellspring of any issues. This guarantees item quality as well as helps in diminishing waste and further developing proficiency.

Endeavor asset arranging (ERP) frameworks have become vital in overseeing producing cycles and detectability. These frameworks incorporate different parts of creation, including stock administration, request handling, and quality control. By giving constant information and experiences, ERP frameworks work with powerful recognizability and assist producers with settling on informed choices.

The car business is a great representation of the assembling area where detectability is central. Vehicles comprise of thousands of parts from various providers, making it vital for follow the wellspring of each part. Auto makers use standardized identifications and RFID labels to distinguish and follow parts all through the gathering system. This guarantees that deficient or rebellious parts can be immediately distinguished and supplanted, working on the general quality and security of the vehicles.

The reception of Industry 4.0 standards, which incorporate the utilization of IoT gadgets and sensors, has additionally upgraded recognizability in assembling. These gadgets give constant information on apparatus execution, item quality, and cycle proficiency. Makers can utilize this information to screen and enhance their activities, diminishing waste and further developing item quality.

Innovation and detectability arrangements offer various advantages to organizations and enterprises, including upgraded straightforwardness, worked on quality control, expanded security, and smoothed out activities. Nonetheless, their execution additionally accompanies difficulties and contemplations that should be tended to.

Chapter 7

Mindful Eating and Nutrition

Careful eating is a training that has acquired critical consideration lately as individuals look to lay out better associations with food and further develop their general prosperity. It includes giving close consideration to the demonstration of eating, zeroing in on the tactile experience, and developing a more profound association with the food being devoured. In this paper, we will investigate the idea of careful eating, its standards, and its effect on nourishment, wellbeing, and in general way of life.

Careful eating is established in the way of thinking of care, a training that underlines being available at the time and completely captivating with one's encounters, contemplations, and sentiments. When applied to eating, it urges people to turn out to be more receptive to the demonstration of devouring food, taking into consideration a more profound enthusiasm for the flavors, surfaces, and sensations related with eating.

One of the fundamental standards of careful eating is eating with goal. This implies settling on cognizant decisions about what, when, and the amount to eat, as opposed to carelessly devouring food without really thinking or because of outside signals like pressure, weariness, or prevailing burden. It includes paying attention to the body's craving and completion signs and pursuing choices in light of physical and profound necessities.

One more fundamental part of careful eating is relishing the tactile experience of food. This incorporates focusing on the taste, surface, and smell of each nibble. By completely submerging oneself in the eating experience, people can acquire a more prominent appreciation for the food and get additional fulfillment from it. This, thusly, can diminish the inclination to thoughtlessly gorge or devour food.

Careful eating additionally supports the act of eating gradually and appreciating each chomp. This purposeful speed permits people to see when they are starting to feel full, keeping them from gorging. It likewise gives the body time to enlist the utilization of food, which can prompt a more noteworthy feeling of satiety and satisfaction with more modest parts.

Besides, careful eating accentuates the significance of being in line with appetite and completion signals. As opposed to eating as per a foreordained timetable or outer signals, people are urged to pay attention to their bodies and eat when they are eager. Additionally, they are encouraged to quit eating when they are fulfilled, as opposed to when the plate is unfilled.

Integrating care into supper time can be an extraordinary encounter, as it permits people to break liberated from undesirable eating designs and foster a more certain relationship with food. This training can prompt different advantages connected with sustenance, wellbeing, and generally speaking prosperity.

One of the essential benefits of careful eating is advancing better food choices potential. At the point when people become more aware of what they are eating and why, they are bound to pick food varieties that are supporting and fulfilling. This can prompt an eating regimen wealthy in entire, natural food varieties, organic products, vegetables, and lean proteins, while diminishing the utilization of profoundly handled and undesirable choices.

Careful eating can likewise be an important device for weight the board. By focusing on craving and completion prompts, people are less inclined to gorge or consume over the top calories. This can add to weight reduction or weight upkeep, as careful eaters are more sensitive to their bodies' regular guideline of food admission.

Besides, careful eating has been related with a decrease in profound eating. Close to home eating frequently includes devouring food as a method for adapting to pressure, misery, weariness, or other profound triggers. By rehearsing careful eating, people can turn out to be more mindful of their feelings and foster elective methodologies for overseeing them, lessening the dependence on nourishment for solace.

The advantages of careful eating likewise reach out to absorption. At the point when people eat food carefully, they are bound to bite their food completely, which helps with the underlying phases of absorption. Appropriate biting can assist with forestalling stomach related uneasiness, for example, bulging and acid reflux, and may prompt superior supplement retention.

Moreover, careful eating can upgrade the general fulfillment got from dinners. By relishing each chomp and completely captivating with the eating experience, people might find that they need less food to feel fulfilled. This can prompt a more prominent feeling of satisfaction and satisfaction from feasts, in any event, while consuming more modest segments.

On the mental and profound front, careful eating can add to a better relationship with food and self-perception. It energizes self-empathy and self-acknowledgment, assisting people with relinquishing culpability or disgrace related with eating. This change in outlook can decrease tension and stress connected with food decisions and advance a more sure mental self portrait.

Moreover, careful eating can further develop consciousness of desires and craving. By being sensitive to the actual impressions of appetite and completion, people can separate between certified hunger and different kinds of desires, like fatigue or close to home triggers. This mindfulness takes into consideration more cognizant choices about when and what to eat.

Careful eating likewise can possibly cultivate a superior comprehension of the mental elements that impact eating ways of behaving. It urges people to ponder the hidden explanations behind their eating designs, assisting them with distinguishing triggers or stressors that might prompt unfortunate decisions. This mindfulness can prompt the advancement of better methods for dealing with hardship or stress.

Notwithstanding the singular advantages, careful eating can add to additional positive social and social perspectives toward food. By cultivating an appreciation for the tangible experience of eating and advancing appreciation for the accessibility of sustaining food, careful eating can reshape the manner in which society perspectives and values food.

While careful eating offers various benefits, it is fundamental to recognize that it's anything but a one-size-fits-all arrangement. The training may not be appropriate for everybody, and its adequacy can differ from one individual to another. A few people might find it trying to incorporate care into their dietary patterns because of different variables, including time imperatives, social impacts, or individual inclinations.

Moreover, careful eating may not be an independent answer for people with specific ailments or explicit dietary necessities. Those with ailments that require severe dietary rules, like diabetes or food sensitivities, ought to work with medical care experts to guarantee that their dietary necessities are met while consolidating careful eating standards.

Moreover, careful eating may not generally be proper for people battling with dietary issues, for example, anorexia nervosa or bulimia. In such cases, the emphasis ought to be on resolving the basic mental and intense subject matters through specific therapy and treatment.

All in all, careful eating is a training that urges people to move toward their relationship with food with more prominent mindfulness, aim, and appreciation. By focusing on the tangible experience of eating, paying attention to craving and completion signals, and being receptive to profound triggers, people can change their dietary patterns and foster a more sure association with food.

Careful eating offers various advantages, including the advancement of better food decisions, weight the executives, diminished profound eating, further developed processing, and a more sure relationship with food and self-perception. It can possibly influence people as well as the more extensive social and cultural perspectives toward food.

Nonetheless, it is essential to perceive that careful eating is definitely not a one-size-fits-all arrangement, and its viability can change from one individual to another. It may not be reasonable for people with specific ailments or those battling with dietary problems. The act of careful eating ought to be custom-made to individual necessities and conditions, and people ought to look for proficient direction when important to guarantee that their dietary prerequisites and wellbeing concerns are fittingly tended to.

7.1 Promoting mindful eating habits

Advancing careful dietary patterns is fundamental in a world portrayed by speedy ways of life, a wealth of handled food sources, and a rising spotlight on outside signals for eating. Careful eating is a training that urges people to reconnect with the experience of eating by being completely present, focusing on the tangible parts of food, and pursuing cognizant decisions about what, when, and how to eat. In this exposition, we will investigate methodologies for advancing careful dietary patterns, their advantages, and the likely moves and boundaries to their reception.

Instructive Drives: One of the best ways of advancing careful dietary patterns is through instructive drives that bring issues to light about the training. Schools, people group associations, and medical services suppliers can offer studios and seminars on careful eating, giving people the information and abilities to integrate this training into their lives. These drives can cover subjects, for example, the standards of careful eating, the advantages it offers, and useful procedures for carrying out it.

Virtual Entertainment and Online Assets: Utilizing the force of web-based entertainment and online stages can be a successful method for contacting a wide crowd. Blog entries, recordings, and web-based entertainment missions can share data about careful eating and give tips and assets to those keen on embracing the training. These stages can likewise cultivate a feeling of local area and backing for people on their careful eating venture.

Medical care Experts: Medical services suppliers, including dietitians, nutritionists, and specialists, assume an essential part in advancing careful dietary patterns. They can incorporate careful eating into their advising and treatment meetings, giving direction and customized techniques to clients. Doctors can likewise underscore the significance of careful eating in overseeing ailments connected with diet, like diabetes or weight.

Corporate Health Projects: Businesses can add to advancing careful eating by offering wellbeing programs that remember training for the training. Health drives can give representatives apparatuses and assets to integrate care into their day to day schedules, at last further developing their general prosperity and efficiency. Working environment cafeterias can likewise offer careful food decisions and urge representatives to relish their feasts.

Culinary Instruction: Culinary schools and cooking classes can integrate careful eating into their educational plans. Helping people to plan dinners with aim and to relish the flavors and surfaces of food can ingrain careful dietary patterns starting from the earliest stage. These abilities can prompt better eating designs and a more profound appreciation for the culinary expressions.

Nurturing and Family Commitment: Empowering careful eating in families is fundamental for advancing these propensities since early on. Guardians and parental figures can act as good examples by rehearsing careful eating themselves. Drawing in youngsters in feast planning and teaching them about the significance of focusing on their food can lay out long lasting smart dieting propensities.

Careful Eating Applications: In the computerized age, there are various cell phone applications intended to help careful eating. These applications can give directed contemplations, suggestions to eat carefully, and apparatuses for following eating ways of behaving. Clients can profit from the comfort of having careful eating assets readily available, making it simpler to integrate the training into their day to day schedules.

Careful Eating Difficulties: Associations, schools, and networks can arrange careful eating difficulties or occasions. These moves can urge people to rehearse careful eating for a predefined period, like a week or a month. Members can share their encounters, experiences, and progress, encouraging a feeling of local area and responsibility.

Careful Eating and Nourishment Studios: Facilitating studios that consolidate sustenance schooling with careful eating standards can offer a comprehensive way to deal with good dieting. These studios can give members the information and instruments to make educated, careful decisions about their eating regimens. They can figure out how to perceive yearning and completion prompts, distinguish close to home eating triggers, and pick food varieties that feed their bodies.

Support Gatherings: Making or taking part in help bunches zeroed in on careful eating can offer a feeling of local area and shared encounters. Individuals can share difficulties, victories, and systems for integrating careful eating into their lives. This social help can assist people with remaining propelled and focused on the training.

The advantages of advancing careful dietary patterns are critical and incorporate different parts of physical and mental prosperity:

Further developed Sustenance: Careful eating urges people to go with additional cognizant and informed decisions about the food varieties they devour. By focusing on their bodies' craving and completion signals, people are bound to eat as per their wholesome necessities, bringing about an eating routine that is adjusted and feeding.

Weight The executives: Careful eating has been related with better weight the board. By encouraging consciousness of part sizes and decreasing indulging, people are bound to keep a solid weight or lose overabundance weight if necessary. Careful eating likewise advances a better relationship with food, lessening the probability of prohibitive or gorging designs.

Upgraded Processing: Biting food completely and eating at a moderate speed, as supported by careful eating, can further develop assimilation. Sufficient biting takes into account better breakdown of food, making it more straightforward for the stomach related framework to process and assimilate supplements.

Stress Decrease: Careful eating advances unwinding and diminishes pressure around supper time. At the point when people are completely present and zeroed in on their food, they are more averse to race through dinners or experience uneasiness connected with eating. This can add to better absorption and by and large prosperity.

Profound Guideline: Careful eating can assist people with recognizing close to home triggers for eating and foster better survival methods. It supports mindfulness and self-empathy, lessening close to home eating and encouraging a more certain relationship with food.

Further developed Self-perception: Rehearsing careful eating can prompt a better self-perception. By relinquishing culpability or disgrace related with eating, people can foster a more certain mental self portrait and a more prominent identity acknowledgment.

Upgraded Satisfaction in Food: Appreciating the tangible experience of eating improves the general pleasure in food. Careful eaters frequently find that they get more prominent fulfillment from their feasts, in any event, while consuming more modest bits.

Worked on Emotional well-being: The act of care, which is at the center of careful eating, has been connected to worked on emotional wellness. Care can lessen side effects of tension, despondency, and stress, adding to a more sure and adjusted close to home state.

Positive Social and Social Effect: Advancing careful eating can move cultural perspectives toward food, empowering a more prominent appreciation for the tangible experience of eating and a more comprehensive way to deal with sustenance. This can prompt a culture that qualities and regards food in a better manner.

Notwithstanding the various advantages of advancing careful dietary patterns, a few difficulties and boundaries might block its reception and coordination into day to day existence:

Speedy Ways of life: Numerous people have occupied existences with chaotic timetables, allowing for careful dinner planning and utilization. The strain to eat rapidly and in a hurry can impede the act of careful eating.

Social and Social Impacts: Social standards and social assumptions can assume a huge part in eating ways of behaving. In certain societies, shared and high speed dinners might put the act of careful eating down. Prevalent burdens to eat explicit food varieties or follow specific eating examples can likewise be trying to explore.

Outer Prompts and Interruptions: Current living is frequently loaded up with outside signals and interruptions that pull people from the current second. Innovation, business related pressure, and steady network can make it hard to zero in on the demonstration of eating.

Profound Dietary patterns: Close to home eating, frequently determined by pressure, weariness, or profound triggers, can be a huge obstruction to taking on careful dietary patterns. Bringing an end to liberated from these propensities and tracking down better ways of adapting to feelings can challenge.

Restricted Availability to Entire Food varieties: Financial variables, including admittance to reasonable and nutritious entire food varieties, can influence a singular's capacity to rehearse careful eating. Restricted admittance to new deliver and entire grains might prompt dependence on handled and less fortifying choices.

Protection from Change: Change can be testing, and people might be impervious to embracing new dietary patterns, particularly in the event that they have longstanding examples of eating conduct. The solace and commonality of laid out schedules can impede the reception of careful eating.

Misinterpretations and Deception: Misguided judgments about careful eating might deter people from investigating the training. For instance, some might see it as excessively prohibitive or a type of counting calories, as opposed to an all encompassing way to deal with food and prosperity.

Absence of Mindfulness: A few people may essentially know nothing about the idea of careful eating and its possible advantages. They might not have had the valuable chance to find out about the training or get direction on the best way to integrate it into their lives.

7.2 Access to nutritious food options

Admittance to nutritious food choices is a basic part of general wellbeing, and it assumes a huge part in deciding the prosperity of people and networks. The accessibility and reasonableness of quality food sources are fundamental for advancing a decent eating routine and forestalling diet-related medical problems. In this article, we will investigate the significance of admittance to nutritious food, the variables that impact it, and the results of restricted admittance in different networks.

Significance of Admittance to Nutritious Food:

Admittance to nutritious food is an essential common freedom and a foundation of general wellbeing. It is fundamental because of multiple factors:

Supplement Admission: Admittance to nutritious food sources guarantees that people get the fundamental supplements, nutrients, and minerals their bodies need to appropriately work. A fair eating routine wealthy in natural products, vegetables, entire grains, lean proteins, and solid fats is related with lower dangers of persistent sicknesses like coronary illness, diabetes, and particular sorts of malignant growth.

Development and Advancement: For youngsters and teenagers, admittance to nutritious food is urgent for sound development and improvement. Appropriate nourishment upholds actual development, mental turn of events, and in general prosperity. Insufficient admittance to nutritious food sources can prompt formative postponements and long lasting wellbeing challenges.

Emotional well-being: Sustenance assumes a huge part in emotional wellness. An eating routine wealthy in supplements is related with further developed mind-set, mental capability, and mental prosperity. Interestingly, an absence of admittance to nutritious food can add to emotional wellness issues, including sadness and tension.

Counteraction of Diet-Related Sicknesses: Restricted admittance to nutritious food can bring about an overreliance on handled and unfortunate choices, prompting an expanded gamble of diet-related infections. This incorporates conditions like corpulence, hypertension, and type 2 diabetes.

Decreased Medical services Expenses: By elevating admittance to nutritious food, society can lessen the weight on medical services frameworks. Forestalling diet-related infections through appropriate sustenance can bring down medical care costs and further develop by and large populace wellbeing.

Factors Impacting Admittance to Nutritious Food:

A few variables impact admittance to nutritious food, and these elements can fluctuate fundamentally by area, financial status, and individual conditions:

Pay and Moderateness: Quite possibly of the most basic variable influencing admittance to nutritious food is pay. Low-pay people and families frequently battle to manage the cost of solid choices. Supplement thick food sources like new products of the soil, lean proteins, and entire grains are in many cases more costly than calorie-thick, handled food varieties.

Geographic Area: The actual area of people and networks can likewise affect their admittance to nutritious food. "Food deserts" are regions where there is restricted admittance to supermarkets or markets that offer various new and quality food sources. These regions are much of the time tracked down in low-pay areas and rustic networks.

Transportation: Admittance to nutritious food is firmly connected to transportation choices. People without admittance to a solid vehicle might battle to arrive at supermarkets or markets that offer sound decisions. This can prompt an overreliance on adjacent odds and ends shops, which might have restricted nutritious choices.

Food Accessibility and Appropriation: The accessibility of nutritious food can change fundamentally contingent upon the area. In certain areas, there might be a wealth of new produce and entire food varieties, while in others, there might be restricted accessibility. The conveyance of food choices inside a local area can be impacted by monetary factors and market elements.

Social and Social Variables: Social inclinations and accepted practices can impact food decisions. Admittance to nutritious food might be obliged by social inclinations for specific sorts of cooking or an absence of familiarity with better other options.

Information and Instruction: Restricted information about nourishment and good food decisions can influence admittance to nutritious food. People who don't know about the advantages of a fair eating routine might be less roused to search out and consume nutritious choices.

Government Strategies and Food Projects: Government approaches assume a huge part in forming admittance to nutritious food. Programs like the Supplemental

Nourishment Help Program (SNAP) in the US expect to give monetary help to low-pay people and families, assisting them with managing the cost of better food varieties. Arrangements connected with agribusiness and food creation can likewise affect the accessibility and cost of nutritious choices.

Results of Restricted Admittance to Nutritious Food:

The results of restricted admittance to nutritious food are colossal and have critical ramifications for individual and general wellbeing:

Healthful Lacks: Restricted admittance to nutritious food can bring about wholesome inadequacies. People might miss the mark on nutrients and minerals, which can prompt medical problems like frailty, nutrient inadequacies, and compromised invulnerable capability.

Expanded Hazard of Constant Illnesses: An eating routine that is high in calorie-thick, handled food varieties and low in nutritious choices builds the gamble of persistent sicknesses. Conditions like stoutness, coronary illness, type 2 diabetes, and specific sorts of malignant growth are more common in networks with restricted admittance to nutritious food.

Food Weakness: Food instability, characterized as the powerlessness to bear the cost of sufficient nutritious nourishment for a functioning, sound life, is an immediate outcome of restricted admittance. Food frailty is related with poor physical and emotional well-being, as well as financial insecurity.

Wellbeing Incongruities: Restricted admittance to nutritious food is frequently connected to wellbeing differences. Low-pay networks and networks of variety are lopsidedly impacted, encountering higher paces of diet-related infections and more unfortunate wellbeing results.

Emotional wellness Effect: Wholesome lacks coming about because of restricted admittance to nutritious food can likewise affect psychological well-being. An eating routine coming up short on fundamental supplements can add to despondency, tension, and other psychological well-being issues.

Instructive and Financial Results: Youngsters who experience food frailty because of restricted admittance to nutritious food might confront instructive difficulties, including trouble thinking and lower scholarly accomplishment. Furthermore, food weakness can propagate patterns of destitution and monetary precariousness.

Addressing Restricted Admittance to Nutritious Food:

Addressing restricted admittance to nutritious food requires a complete and complex methodology:

Monetary Intercessions: Executing arrangements that address pay imbalance and offer monetary help to low-pay people and families can further develop admittance to nutritious food. Drives like expanding the lowest pay permitted by law, extending the Acquired Personal Tax reduction (EITC), and fortifying social security nets can lighten monetary hindrances to smart dieting.

Local area Based Arrangements: Nearby people group can make a move by laying out local area plants, ranchers' business sectors, and food cooperatives. These drives can give admittance to new, privately obtained, and reasonable nutritious food choices.

Transportation Access: Further developing transportation choices in regions with restricted admittance to nutritious food is fundamental. This might include upgrading public transportation, carrying out versatile food showcases, or advancing carpooling and rideshare programs.

Nourishment Schooling: Giving training about sustenance and quality food decisions is significant. This can be accomplished through school educational programs, local area studios, and general wellbeing efforts. Information about the advantages of a decent eating routine can engage people to pursue better decisions.

Government Strategies: Government approaches at the bureaucratic, state, and neighborhood levels can altogether affect admittance to nutritious food. This incorporates arrangements connected with food help programs, appropriations for farming, and guidelines on food publicizing to kids.

Joint effort and Support: Cooperation among government offices, non-benefit associations, medical care suppliers, and local area pioneers is fundamental. Backing endeavors can bring issues to light of the significance of addressing restricted admittance to nutritious food and drive strategy changes.

7.3 The link between Farm to Fork and improved health

The "Homestead to Fork" model, frequently alluded to as "Ranch to Table" or "Homestead to Plate," is a comprehensive way to deal with food creation and dispersion that underlines the immediate association between the wellspring of food (cultivates) and its utilization (tables or plates). This approach has picked up speed as of late because of further developing wellbeing results for people and communities potential. In this exposition, we will investigate the connection between the Homestead to Fork model and further developed wellbeing, looking at the different manners by which this approach can emphatically affect sustenance, general wellbeing, and by and large prosperity.

1. **Further developed Nourishment:**

One of the essential manners by which the Ranch to Fork model upgrades wellbeing is by further developing nourishment. By shortening the store network and interfacing customers straightforwardly to neighborhood ranches and food makers, this approach advances the utilization of new, occasional, and privately obtained food sources. This significantly affects nourishment:

1. **Expanded Utilization of New Produce:** Ranch to Fork empowers the utilization of new leafy foods, which are plentiful in fundamental nutrients, minerals,

and dietary fiber. An eating routine high in new produce is related with decreased hazard of constant sicknesses, including coronary illness and particular sorts of disease.

2. **Occasional Assortment:** Embracing occasional food sources guarantees a different and supplement rich eating regimen. Occasional produce is commonly at its top concerning flavor and dietary benefit, making it an important expansion to dinners.

3. **Diminished Handled Food sources:** By accentuating entire, natural food sources, the Homestead to Fork model decreases the admission of handled and profoundly refined items, which are in many cases high in undesirable fats, added sugars, and counterfeit added substances.

4. **Lower Sodium and Sugar Admission:** Many handled food varieties are famous for their high sodium and sugar content. Accentuating new, privately obtained fixings permits people to control and lessen their admission of these unsafe substances.

2. Expanded Food Mindfulness:

Homestead to Fork urges people to be more aware of where their food comes from, the way things are developed or raised, and the excursion it takes from the ranch to the table. This elevated mindfulness has a few wellbeing related benefits:

1. **Grasping Food Quality:** When people have an immediate association with neighborhood homesteads and food makers, they can acquire experiences into cultivating rehearses, food quality, and the shortfall of destructive synthetic substances or added substances. This information engages customers to settle on informed decisions about the food varieties they eat.

2. **Cognizant Food Decisions:** An attention to the wellspring of food and the cultivating strategies utilized can prompt more cognizant food decisions. This incorporates choices to help supportable and harmless to the ecosystem rural practices, as well as the evasion of food items that add to deforestation, natural surroundings obliteration, or unreasonable utilization of pesticides.

3. **Worked on Dietary Propensities:** A superior comprehension of the starting points of food can prompt better dietary propensities. People might be bound to keep away from food items related with deceptive or impractical practices, like those connected with creature government assistance or ecological preservation.

3. Reinforced Neighborhood Economies:

The Ranch to Fork model frequently advances neighborhood and territorial food frameworks, supporting nearby ranchers and food makers. This fortifies neighborhood economies and has circuitous medical advantages:

1. **Monetary Soundness:** Supporting nearby ranchers and food makers can reinforce the financial strength of country and agrarian networks. Solid nearby economies add to further developed admittance to medical care, training, and different administrations that influence general wellbeing.

2. **Work Creation:** Neighborhood food frameworks make occupations, both on ranches and in the food creation and dissemination areas. Business open doors can further develop the monetary prosperity of networks, diminishing neediness rates and related wellbeing abberations.

4. Decreased Ecological Effect:

Homestead to Fork underscores supportable and harmless to the ecosystem agrarian practices. This emphatically affects general wellbeing through:

1. **Decreased Compound Openness:** Feasible cultivating rehearses frequently limit the utilization of manufactured pesticides and composts. This decreases synthetic deposits on food items, bringing the gamble of openness down to unsafe substances.

2. **Biodiversity Protection:** Empowering reasonable cultivating rehearses upholds biodiversity preservation. Saving assorted environments and safeguarding pollinators and different species adds to natural equilibrium and long haul wellbeing.

5. Local area Building:

The Ranch to Fork model cultivates local area building and social attachment, which significantly affect wellbeing:

1. **Social Associations:** People group ranchers' business sectors, neighborhood food occasions, and cultivate visits give amazing open doors to social collaboration and association. Solid informal organizations are related with worked on mental and close to home prosperity.

2. **Feeling of Having a place:** Contribution in nearby food drives makes a feeling of having a place and shared character inside networks. This can diminish sensations of segregation and depression, which are connected to psychological wellness issues.

6. Instruction and Mindfulness:

Ranch to Fork drives frequently include instructive parts that assist people with creating food-related information and abilities. This can further develop wellbeing results through:

1. **Nourishment Training:** Instructive projects related with the Homestead to Fork model can improve sustenance information and dietary ways of behaving, assisting people with pursuing better food decisions.
2. **Cooking Abilities:** Figuring out how to get ready and cook new, entire food sources can prompt better feast readiness at home, diminishing the dependence on handled and quick food sources.
3. **Food Education:** Acquiring information about the sources and dietary benefit of food advances food proficiency, empowering people to settle on informed decisions for them as well as their families.

Difficulties and Contemplations:

While the Ranch to Fork model offers various medical advantages, a few difficulties and contemplations should be addressed to expand its true capacity:

1. **Availability:** Guaranteeing that Homestead to Fork drives are open to all people, paying little heed to pay or area, is fundamental. Resolving issues connected with food deserts and transportation obstructions is pivotal.
2. **Moderateness:** Neighborhood and natural food varieties can be more costly than their ordinary partners. Endeavors to make nutritious, privately obtained food sources more reasonable are important to defeat this test.
3. **Food handling:** Keeping up with sanitation norms is fundamental while advancing nearby and reasonable food frameworks. Schooling on safe food dealing with and straightforward stock chains can assist with building trust in these frameworks.
4. **Value and Inclusivity:** Endeavors should be made to guarantee that all networks approach the advantages of the Ranch to Fork model. Procedures ought to be carried out to address food equity and food sway issues.
5. **Increasing:** Extending the Ranch to Fork model to arrive at a bigger piece of the populace while keeping up with its standards of neighborhood, reasonable, and moral food creation can be a perplexing test.

Chapter 8

Informed Consumer Choices

Informed purchaser decisions are the foundation of a flourishing and impartial commercial center. In the present interconnected world, where purchasers are assaulted with a staggering exhibit of choices, settling on informed choices has never been more critical. This isn't just essential for people trying to get the best incentive for their well deserved cash, yet it likewise has expansive ramifications for the economy, the climate, and society in general. In this article, we will investigate the meaning of informed shopper decisions, the difficulties customers face, and the devices and methodologies accessible to enable buyers to pursue more educated choices.

Purchaser decisions assume a critical part in the working of any market. The choices people make while buying labor and products straightforwardly affect the achievement or disappointment of organizations. Organizations endeavor to comprehend customer inclinations and patterns to fulfill the needs of their main interest group. In any case, for customers to pursue informed decisions, they should be furnished with information and data about the items and administrations they are thinking about. Without this information, buyers are in a difficult spot, making it hard to really explore the mind boggling commercial center.

One of the essential justifications for why informed shopper decisions are fundamental is that they add to a more effective market. An effective market is one where costs precisely mirror the market interest for labor and products. At the point when purchasers approach exhaustive data, they can pursue choices that line up with their requirements and inclinations, which thus, impacts market elements. Costs change in light of buyer conduct, and organizations are boosted to offer better quality items and administrations at serious costs. This opposition drives development and prompts further developed items and administrations.

Informed purchaser decisions likewise significantly affect the climate. In a time where maintainability and natural worries are principal, buyers have the ability to pursue eco-accommodating decisions. By picking items that are morally created, feasible, and eco-cognizant, customers can add to a more dependable and harmless to the ecosystem commercial center. This, thus, urges organizations to take on more harmless to the ecosystem works on, diminishing their carbon impression and generally speaking effect in the world.

Additionally, educated purchaser decisions are instrumental in molding the social scene. By deciding to help organizations that maintain moral and social obligation guidelines, purchasers can empower positive corporate way of behaving. Organizations that focus on fair work practices, variety and consideration, and local area commitment are bound to flourish in a general public where informed shoppers prize such qualities with their support. This dynamic supports the idea that shopper decisions are monetary choices as well as moral and social proclamations.

Be that as it may, going with informed buyer decisions isn't generally a direct errand. Purchasers face various difficulties in their quest for information and data. One of the essential hindrances is the staggering volume of decisions accessible on the lookout. With the appearance of web based business and worldwide stock chains, purchasers are given an overflow of items and administrations, making it trying to separate between them. The sheer assortment of choices can prompt choice loss of motion, where shoppers can't pursue decisions with certainty.

Furthermore, customers frequently experience deceiving publicizing and promoting strategies that make it challenging to perceive the genuine worth and nature of an item or administration. Organizations concentrate on making convincing promoting efforts, and purchasers might wind up influenced by genuinely engaging messages instead of true data. This can prompt purchaser's regret when buyers find that their buys don't satisfy the showcasing publicity.

The absence of straightforwardness in supply chains and creation processes further entangles purchaser direction. Numerous buyers are worried about the moral and natural ramifications of the items they buy. In any case, getting data about an item's starting points and creation strategies can challenge, as organizations may not necessarily unveil these subtleties deliberately.

Notwithstanding these difficulties, purchasers might miss the mark on fundamental monetary proficiency to settle on informed decisions about monetary items and administrations. The universe of individual budget is mind boggling, with a heap of choices for reserve funds, speculations, credits, and protection. Without a solid comprehension of monetary standards and the likely dangers and prizes, shoppers might pursue choices that have long haul monetary outcomes.

The computerized age has acquainted new aspects with the difficulties purchasers face. Internet shopping and web based business stages have upset the manner in which individuals shop, offering comfort and an immense choice. Be that as it may, this advanced change likewise brings new dangers, for example, online tricks, information breaks, and the spread of fake items. In the web-based space, purchasers should practice mindfulness and network safety attention to shield themselves from different web-based dangers.

Notwithstanding these difficulties, there are devices and procedures accessible to enable shoppers to pursue more educated decisions. One of the most basic devices is instruction. Purchaser schooling is fundamental for fostering the information and abilities expected to effectively explore the market. Instructive drives, both formal and casual, can assist shoppers with turning out to be seriously knowing and basic in their navigation. This incorporates understanding how to decipher item names, analyze costs, and recognize tricky publicizing rehearses.

Unofficial laws and purchaser security regulations likewise assume a crucial part in guaranteeing that buyers approach precise and straightforward data. These guidelines expect organizations to uncover fundamental insights regarding their items and administrations, including fixings, healthful data, wellbeing alerts, and natural effect. By upholding such guidelines, legislatures assist with making everything fair and shield purchasers from fake or unsafe practices.

Purchaser support associations are one more imperative asset for enabling informed decisions. These associations work to address the interests of shoppers and consider organizations responsible for their activities. They give data, lead examination, and promoter for approaches that safeguard purchaser privileges. Through crafted by these associations, purchasers can get to important data and assets to go with informed choices.

The ascent of online audits and evaluations stages has additionally changed the manner in which purchasers accumulate data about items and administrations. Destinations like Cry, TripAdvisor, and Amazon surveys permit purchasers to peruse the encounters and assessments of other people who have utilized a specific item or administration. These stages give significant bits of knowledge into this present reality execution and nature of what is being advertised. Nonetheless, purchasers should in any case practice alert, as phony surveys and controlled appraisals can exist.

Mechanical advancements have led to different applications and online apparatuses intended to help shoppers in settling on informed decisions. Cost correlation sites, for example, assist buyers with looking at the costs of comparable items from various retailers. Applications and sites that track item reviews and wellbeing cautions assist purchasers with remaining informed about possibly hurtful items. Also, blockchain innovation holds the possibility to give straightforward and changeless store network data, empowering shoppers to follow the beginning and excursion of items they buy.

The force of virtual entertainment can't be undervalued with regards to informed buyer decisions. Online entertainment stages permit customers to share their encounters and complaints, possibly considering organizations responsible for their activities. A viral grievance or recognition via virtual entertainment can fundamentally affect an organization's standing. This newly discovered capacity for shoppers to by and large voice their perspectives can drive organizations to work on their items and administrations.

Informed purchaser decisions additionally reach out to the monetary domain. Monetary education projects and assets are fundamental for people to arrive at informed conclusions about investment funds, speculations, and credits. These projects teach buyers on points, for example, planning, understanding loan fees, and the dangers related with different monetary instruments. Information in this space is urgent for guaranteeing one's monetary prosperity and security.

The idea of moral commercialization has picked up speed lately. Moral buyers settle on decisions that line up with their qualities, whether it's supporting fair exchange, harmless to the ecosystem items, or organizations that focus on friendly obligation. Moral commercialization can drive organizations to take on additional moral and economical practices, as they answer the requests of a developing portion of socially cognizant purchasers.

8.1 Empowering consumers with knowledge

Engaging shoppers with information is a critical figure cultivating a more straightforward and evenhanded commercial center. In the cutting edge world, where customers are given a heap of decisions in each part of their lives, it is critical to guarantee that people approach the data they need to settle on informed choices. In this exposition, we will dive into the meaning of engaging customers with information, the difficulties they face in getting that information, and the systems and devices accessible to work with this strengthening.

Buyer strengthening through information is essential since it frames the bedrock of a working business sector economy. Informed buyers drive rivalry by settling on decisions that line up with their necessities and inclinations. At the point when shoppers approach extensive data, they can pursue choices that guide market elements. Organizations are boosted to offer better quality items and administrations at serious costs in light of buyer conduct. This opposition encourages advancement and prompts further developed contributions.

Also, customer strengthening with information has extensive ramifications for the climate. During a time where supportability and natural worries are foremost, customers can assume a huge part in going with eco-accommodating decisions. By choosing items that are morally created, maintainable, and earth cognizant, buyers add to a more dependable and environmentally cordial commercial center. This, thusly, urges organizations to take on more harmless to the ecosystem works on, lessening their effect in the world.

Enabling buyers with information additionally has significant social repercussions. By deciding to help organizations that focus on moral and social obligation norms, purchasers can support positive corporate way of behaving. Organizations that hero fair work practices, variety and consideration, and local area commitment are bound to flourish in a general public where informed purchasers prize such qualities with their support. This dynamic supports that purchaser decisions are not just financial choices but rather additionally moral and social explanations.

All things considered, empowering shoppers to settle on informed decisions isn't generally a direct undertaking. There are various difficulties that buyers experience on their journey for information. One of the essential deterrents is the mind-boggling volume of decisions accessible on the lookout. The approach of internet business and worldwide stock chains has prompted an overflow of items and administrations, making it moving for customers to separate between them. This plenty of choices can prompt choice loss of motion, where purchasers battle to without hesitation decide.

Deceiving publicizing and showcasing strategies represent one more critical test for buyers. Organizations focus intently on making influential promoting efforts, and buyers might end up influenced by genuinely engaging messages instead of true data. This can prompt purchaser's regret when customers understand that their buys don't satisfy the promoting publicity.

The absence of straightforwardness in supply chains and creation processes further confuses customer navigation. Numerous shoppers are worried about the moral and ecological ramifications of the items they buy. Nonetheless, getting data about an item's starting points and creation techniques can challenge, as organizations may not necessarily in every case reveal these subtleties deliberately.

Notwithstanding these difficulties, shoppers might miss the mark on fundamental monetary education to go with informed decisions about monetary items and administrations. The universe of individual budget is intricate, with a horde of choices for reserve funds, speculations, credits, and protection. Without a solid comprehension of monetary standards and the possible dangers and prizes, buyers might pursue choices that have long haul monetary outcomes.

The advanced age has acquainted new aspects with the difficulties shoppers face. Web based shopping and internet business stages have upset the manner in which individuals shop, offering comfort and a tremendous choice. Nonetheless, this computerized change likewise brings new dangers, for example, online tricks, information breaks, and the spread of fake items. In the web-based space, customers should practice watchfulness and network safety attention to safeguard themselves from different web-based dangers.

Notwithstanding these difficulties, there are instruments and systems accessible to enable customers with the information expected to pursue more educated decisions. One of the most basic devices is schooling.

Shopper training is fundamental for fostering the information and abilities expected to effectively explore the market. Instructive drives, both formal and casual, can assist shoppers with turning out to be really knowing and basic in their navigation. This incorporates understanding how to decipher item names, analyze costs, and distinguish tricky promoting rehearses.

Unofficial laws and shopper security regulations likewise assume a critical part in guaranteeing that purchasers approach exact and straightforward data. These guidelines expect organizations to unveil fundamental insights concerning their items and administrations, including fixings, dietary data, security admonitions, and natural effect. By implementing such guidelines, states assist with making everything fair and shield shoppers from false or destructive practices.

Purchaser promotion associations are one more fundamental asset for engaging customers with information. These associations work to address the interests of customers and consider organizations responsible for their activities. They give data, direct examination, and supporter for approaches that safeguard customer freedoms. Through crafted by these associations, shoppers can get to important data and assets to settle on informed choices.

The ascent of online audits and appraisals stages has additionally changed the manner in which buyers accumulate data about items and administrations. Locales like Cry, TripAdvisor, and Amazon surveys permit buyers to peruse the encounters and assessments of other people who have utilized a specific item or administration. These stages give important bits of knowledge into this present reality execution and nature of what is being advertised. In any case, purchasers should in any case practice alert, as phony surveys and controlled evaluations can exist.

Mechanical advancements have led to different applications and online apparatuses intended to help shoppers in settling on informed decisions. Cost correlation sites, for example, assist customers with contrasting the costs of comparable items from various retailers. Applications and sites that track item reviews and wellbeing alarms assist buyers with remaining informed about possibly hurtful items. Also, blockchain innovation holds the possibility to give straightforward and permanent store network data, empowering shoppers to follow the beginning and excursion of items they buy.

The force of virtual entertainment can't be undervalued with regards to engaging buyers with information. Virtual entertainment stages permit customers to share their encounters and complaints, possibly considering organizations responsible for their activities. A viral objection or recognition via web-based entertainment can essentially affect an organization's standing. This newly discovered capacity for customers to all in all voice their perspectives can drive organizations to work on their items and administrations.

Informed buyer decisions additionally reach out to the monetary domain. Monetary education projects and assets are fundamental for people to settle on informed conclusions about reserve funds, ventures, and credits. These projects instruct customers on subjects, for example, planning, understanding loan fees, and the dangers related with different monetary instruments. Information in this space is vital for guaranteeing one's monetary prosperity and security.

The idea of moral commercialization has picked up speed as of late. Moral shoppers pursue decisions that line up with their qualities, whether it's supporting fair exchange, harmless to the ecosystem items, or organizations that focus on friendly obligation. Moral industrialism can drive organizations to embrace more moral and reasonable practices, as they answer the requests of a developing portion of socially cognizant customers.

8.2 Transparency in food labeling

Straightforwardness in food marking is a fundamental component of current shopper decisions and the food business in general. How food items are marked and introduced to buyers altogether influences their buying choices, wellbeing, and by and large prosperity. In this article, we will investigate the significance of straightforwardness in food naming, the difficulties related with it, and the possible advantages of furnishing shoppers with clear and exact data about the food sources they buy.

Straightforwardness in food marking is vital in light of multiple factors, with the most prompt being purchaser wellbeing and security. The data gave on food names, for example, fixing records and dietary realities, permits shoppers to settle on informed decisions about the items they eat. It assists people with dietary limitations, sensitivities, and other explicit necessities to distinguish reasonable choices, diminishing the gamble of antagonistic responses or medical problems.

Moreover, straightforwardness in food marking is fundamental for keeping up with trust among shoppers and food producers. At the point when buyers accept they are getting precise and legit data about the items they buy, they are bound to trust the brands and organizations behind those items. Trust is a major part of purchaser dependability, and it can essentially influence an organization's standing and long haul achievement.

The requirement for straightforwardness in food marking is enhanced by the rising predominance of diet-related medical problems and way of life related illnesses. Numerous buyers are more wellbeing cognizant and worried about the nourishing substance of the food varieties they eat. Admittance to exact data about carbohydrate levels, macronutrients, nutrients, and minerals engages purchasers to pursue decisions lined up with their wellbeing and dietary objectives. In addition, straightforward naming can add to the counteraction of diet-related sicknesses like heftiness, diabetes, and coronary illness by empowering people to go with better food decisions.

Sensitivities and food responsive qualities are another region where straightforwardness is foremost. For people with food sensitivities, even a modest quantity of an allergenic fixing can have extreme outcomes. Legitimate marking that plainly recognizes potential allergens assists these people with keeping away from items that could cause an unfavorably susceptible response, diminishing the gamble to their wellbeing and prosperity.

On account of strict or social dietary limitations, straightforward food marking is similarly significant. Numerous people comply with explicit dietary rules in view of their strict convictions or social customs. Exact naming permits them to recognize reasonable items, guaranteeing that their dietary decisions line up with their confidence or social practices.

Ecological and moral contemplations are additionally basic in the present food industry. Shoppers who are worried about maintainability and moral treatment of creatures and laborers frequently search out items that line up with these qualities. Straightforward marking can give data about the beginning and creation strategies for the food, permitting customers to pursue decisions that mirror their moral and natural worries.

Regardless of the certain significance of straightforwardness in food marking, there are a few difficulties related with guaranteeing that this straightforwardness is accomplished. One huge test is the intricacy and changeability of the advanced food store network. The excursion of a solitary food item from its source to the customer's plate can include different stages and various entertainers, making it hard to follow and check the data that ought to be introduced on food marks. Now and again, organizations might not have full perceivability into their stock chains, prompting mistakes in naming.

Marking guidelines can likewise differ starting with one country then onto the next, adding a layer of intricacy to the issue. This can prompt disarray and irregularity in how food items are marked when they are imported or traded. For buyers, this fluctuation can be astounding and lead to misinterpretations of item data.

Moreover, tricky promoting strategies, like unclear or deceiving claims, can darken the real essence of an item. Names that promote items as "normal," "natural," or "solid" without clear definitions or administrative oversight can deceive customers. This can make it provoking for buyers to go with truly educated decisions in view of precise data.

A connected issue is the utilization of confounding or complex fixing names that are new to most buyers. While certain fixings are fundamental in light of multiple factors, including protection and flavor improvement, customers might find it hard to comprehend the organization of an item when confronted with an extensive rundown of unrecognizable terms.

The advanced age has presented new difficulties in the domain of food naming. With the ascent of internet business and online food shopping, buyers may not genuinely see the item's mark until it shows up close to home.

In such cases, it is considerably more important that web-based item portrayals and pictures precisely address the item's happy and healthful data. Buyers need to believe that the data gave online is predictable what they will get.

Tending to these difficulties and accomplishing straightforwardness in food marking requires a complex methodology including different partners, including states, the food business, and customers themselves. One of the essential arrangements is to lay out and implement clear and normalized naming guidelines. These guidelines ought to cover viewpoints, for example, fixing records, wholesome realities, allergen admonitions, and cases made on the bundling.

Legislatures play a huge part to play in setting and implementing these guidelines. They can likewise advance worldwide harmonization of naming guidelines to decrease disarray for the two buyers and organizations working in a worldwide market. Also, legislatures can apportion assets for examinations and reviews to guarantee that organizations follow naming guidelines.

Food makers and makers, then again, should focus on giving precise and straightforward data on their items. This includes putting resources into store network perceivability, which can be accomplished through superior following and documentation of fixings and creation processes. Organizations ought to likewise focus on genuine and clear naming over promoting strategies that could misdirect buyers.

Shoppers, as well, can add to the advancement of straightforwardness in food marking. They can effectively search out data about the items they buy, read names, and pose inquiries when they experience muddled or fragmented data. Shopper interest for straightforwardness can boost organizations to further develop their marking rehearses. Virtual entertainment stages likewise offer a method for purchasers to voice their interests, share data, and consider organizations responsible for their naming and showcasing rehearses.

The reception of innovation can additionally upgrade straightforwardness in food naming. Blockchain innovation, for example, can give an unchanging and straightforward record of an item's excursion from its source to the buyer. This innovation can possibly increment inventory network perceivability and empower shoppers to follow the starting points of the items they buy.

Moreover, cell phone applications and increased reality (AR) can be utilized to furnish customers with constant data about items by examining standardized tags or names. Such applications can offer insights concerning wholesome data, allergen admonitions, and the moral and natural parts of an item, assisting customers with pursuing more educated decisions.

8.3 The impact of informed choices

The effect of informed decisions is significant and expansive, influencing people as well as organizations, society, and the more extensive economy. At the point when shoppers pursue decisions in view of precise and complete data, it has a far reaching influence that impacts markets, deeply molds corporate way of behaving, cultivates supportability, and improves individual prosperity. In this exposition, we will investigate the different components of the effect of informed decisions and how they shape our interconnected world.

At the singular level, the effect of informed decisions is most clear in the existences of buyers. At the point when people approach dependable data, they can settle on choices that line up with their inclinations, values, and needs. This, thusly, prompts more noteworthy fulfillment and prosperity. Informed decisions empower people to choose items and administrations that take care of their particular prerequisites, whether it be dietary limitations, wellbeing objectives, or moral contemplations.

For example, when an individual with a gluten prejudice approaches clear food naming showing sans gluten items, they can certainly pick things that won't set off unfriendly wellbeing responses. Likewise, people taking a stab at a better way of life can settle on educated decisions about the wholesome substance regarding the food sources they eat, which is essential for dealing with their weight and in general well-being. Informed decisions engage people to assume command over their prosperity and work on their personal satisfaction.

On a more extensive scale, the effect of informed shopper decisions stretches out to the economy. Proficient business sectors are predicated on customers pursuing choices in view of their inclinations, and this drives rivalry. At the point when purchasers approach far reaching data, organizations are constrained to enhance and offer better quality items and administrations at serious costs. The cutthroat climate cultivates monetary development and urges organizations to consistently improve and adjust to shopper requests.

The impact of informed decisions on the economy additionally reaches out to ventures and occupation markets. At the point when purchasers favor specific items or administrations because of their quality or moral contemplations, it can drive the outcome of organizations that line up with these qualities. For instance, the interest for natural and harmless to the ecosystem items has prompted the development of businesses that focus on manageability, setting out positions and financial open doors in these areas.

Furthermore, the effect of informed shopper decisions goes past individual buys. It can shape the corporate scene by advancing moral and socially capable practices. At the point when customers decide to help organizations that maintain fair work practices, variety and consideration, and local area commitment, they send a strong message to organizations. Organizations that focus on these qualities are bound to flourish, and those that don't may confront reputational and monetary outcomes.

The climate is one more region where the effect of informed decisions is exceptionally huge. Informed purchasers can pursue eco-accommodating decisions that have positive ramifications for the planet. By selecting items that are morally created, feasible, and eco-cognizant, purchasers add to a more dependable and harmless to the ecosystem commercial center. This urges organizations to take on greener practices, decrease their carbon impression, and limit their effect on the climate. Along these lines, informed purchaser decisions assume a significant part in advancing support-ability and tending to natural worries.

In addition, the effect of informed buyer decisions stretches out to social and moral aspects. Purchasers who focus on items and administrations that line up with their qualities add to an all the more socially mindful commercial center. At the point when buyers support organizations that maintain moral principles, for example, fair wages and safe working circumstances, they advocate for positive social change. This dynamic builds up the possibility that shopper decisions are not just monetary choices but rather likewise moral and social articulations.

In the domain of wellbeing and prosperity, informed decisions straightforwardly affect general wellbeing results. For instance, when buyers approach exact nourishing data, they can settle on better dietary decisions. This can impact decreasing the pervasiveness of diet-related medical problems, like corpulence and diabetes. Furthermore, straightforward food naming permits people with food sensitivities or aversions to stay away from items that could hurt their wellbeing. Informed decisions in medical services can likewise prompt improved results, as patients who comprehend their therapy choices and go with choices in view of informed assent are bound to have positive medical services encounters.

Informed decisions likewise have suggestions for monetary prosperity. Monetary proficiency and informed choices about reserve funds, ventures, advances, and protection are critical for accomplishing long haul monetary security. At the point when buyers comprehend the dangers and prizes related with different monetary items and administrations, they are better prepared to pursue choices that help their monetary objectives. Informed decisions in this space can prompt superior monetary results, not so much obligation, but rather more secure retirement arranging.

The effect of informed decisions is obvious in the computerized age, where the web and innovation have changed the manner in which buyers communicate with items and administrations. Online surveys and appraisals stages have enabled customers to share their encounters and impact the standing of organizations. These stages permit buyers to peruse this present reality encounters and assessments of other people who have utilized a specific item or administration, giving significant experiences into their quality and execution. Informed decisions in the advanced space can save buyers from settling on unfortunate buying choices and can likewise direct them toward better choices.

What's more, the impact of informed decisions is amplified by the force of virtual entertainment. Virtual entertainment stages permit customers to impart their insights and encounters with a wide crowd, impacting public discernments and corporate way of behaving.

A solitary viral protest or recognition via web-based entertainment can essentially affect an organization's standing, spurring them to work on their items and administrations. Web-based entertainment enables purchasers to voice their interests and supporter for positive change by and large.

To upgrade the effect of informed decisions, different instruments and methodologies are accessible. Customer schooling is crucial for fostering the information and abilities expected to successfully explore the market. Instructive drives, both formal and casual, can assist purchasers with turning out to be seriously knowing and basic in their direction. This incorporates understanding how to decipher item names, analyze costs, and distinguish tricky promoting rehearses.

Unofficial laws and purchaser security regulations likewise assume a basic part in guaranteeing that shoppers approach precise and straightforward data. These guidelines expect organizations to reveal fundamental insights concerning their items and administrations, like fixings, dietary data, security admonitions, and ecological effect. By upholding such guidelines, states assist with making everything fair and shield buyers from fake or unsafe practices.

Buyer backing associations address the interests of shoppers and consider organizations responsible for their activities. They give data, direct exploration, and supporter for arrangements that safeguard shopper privileges. Through crafted by these associations, buyers can get to significant data and assets to pursue informed choices and address concerns.

Mechanical advancements have led to different applications and online devices intended to help buyers in pursuing informed decisions. Cost correlation sites assist customers with contrasting costs of comparative items from various retailers. Applications and sites that track item reviews and wellbeing cautions keep purchasers informed about possibly destructive items. Furthermore, blockchain innovation can possibly give straightforward and unchanging inventory network data, empowering shoppers to follow the beginning and excursion of items they buy.

Chapter 9

The Future of Farm to Fork

The future of "Homestead to Fork" is a subject of expanding importance as we wrestle with the difficulties of a developing worldwide populace, changing dietary inclinations, and the critical requirement for supportable and versatile food frameworks. This idea, frequently alluded to as "Ranch to Table" or "Field to Plate," addresses an all encompassing way to deal with food creation, dissemination, and utilization. It incorporates the whole food store network, from the second harvests are planted or creatures are raised to where feasts are appreciated by shoppers. The eventual fate of Homestead to Fork holds the commitment of tending to a scope of basic issues, from food security and ecological manageability to general wellbeing and monetary essentialness.

One of the key perspectives that will shape the eventual fate of Homestead to Fork is the requirement for a more supportable and versatile horticultural framework. With a worldwide populace projected to arrive at 9.7 billion by 2050, the interest for food is developing, and creating more food with less resources is fundamental. This challenge requires a shift towards feasible cultivating works on, including accuracy horticulture, natural cultivating, and regenerative farming. Accuracy horticulture, for example, use innovation, for example, GPS and sensors to improve the utilization of assets like water, composts, and pesticides, bringing about better returns and diminished ecological effect. Natural cultivating centers around limiting engineered inputs and advancing soil wellbeing, biodiversity, and normal nuisance control. Regenerative farming means to reestablish and further develop soil wellbeing, improve biodiversity, and sequester carbon through rehearses like cover trimming and diminished culturing.

Later on, these reasonable cultivating practices will turn out to be more boundless as ranchers and agribusinesses perceive the drawn out advantages of decreasing their ecological impression. The reception of supportable practices will be further boosted by government arrangements and guidelines pointed toward moderating the effect of farming on environmental change, water quality, and biodiversity. The eventual fate of Homestead to Fork will see more ranchers and agrarian organizations embracing supportable practices not exclusively to satisfy shopper need yet in addition to line up with worldwide maintainability objectives.

One more basic part representing things to come of Ranch to Fork is the job of innovation and advancement in changing the food production network. Headways in regions like man-made brainpower, blockchain, and sanitation innovation are ready to reform how food is created, dispersed, and devoured. Man-made reasoning (computer based intelligence) and information investigation can assist ranchers with pursuing more educated choices by breaking down information from sensors, satellites, and different sources to streamline crop the executives. This can prompt expanded yields, diminished waste, and better asset the board.

Blockchain innovation can possibly upgrade straightforwardness and detectability in the food production network. By utilizing a decentralized record, buyers can follow the excursion of their food from the ranch to their plate, guaranteeing more prominent responsibility and diminishing the gamble of food extortion or pollution. Sanitation innovation, including sensors and quick testing techniques, will empower quicker recognition of foodborne microbes, decreasing the probability of foodborne diseases and upgrading buyer trust in the wellbeing of the food supply.

In addition, the fate of Homestead to Fork will be set apart by more noteworthy accentuation on metropolitan agribusiness and vertical cultivating. As additional individuals move to urban communities, the interest for privately developed produce will rise. Metropolitan horticulture includes developing food in or close to urban areas, using housetops, empty parcels, and, surprisingly, indoor spaces. Vertical cultivating takes metropolitan horticulture to a higher level by stacking crops in numerous layers, frequently utilizing tank-farming or aeroponic frameworks. These methodologies lessen the ecological impression of food creation, abbreviate supply chains, and guarantee a new and dependable wellspring of produce for metropolitan populaces.

Besides, the fate of Ranch to Fork will see a more prominent spotlight on elective protein sources. As the interest for meat and dairy items keeps on expanding with rising worldwide earnings, it is fundamental to investigate elective protein sources to lessen the ecological effect of regular domesticated animals cultivating. Plant-based proteins, refined meat, and bug based protein are arising as practical choices. Plant-based proteins, for example, those got from soy, peas, and beans, are turning out to be more well known because of their lower ecological impression and medical advantages. Refined meat, delivered from creature cells without the requirement for raising and butchering creatures, can possibly change the meat business by decreasing ozone harming substance outflows and creature languishing. Bug based protein, currently consumed in certain societies, is profoundly supportable and protein-rich.

The fate of Ranch to Fork will likewise be portrayed by the expanded utilization of food squander decrease systems. Food squander is a huge issue, with roughly 33% of all food created worldwide going to squander. This not just addresses a lost an open door to take care of individuals yet in addition adds to ozone depleting substance outflows. Creative arrangements, for example, food salvage programs, surplus food re-arrangement, and buyer training, will assume a pivotal part in limiting food squander all through the store network.

Furthermore, the fate of Ranch to Fork will focus on the wellbeing and prosperity of shoppers. As individuals become more wellbeing cognizant, there will be a more prominent interest for supplement thick, insignificantly handled food sources. This pattern is supposed to drive changes in both food creation and naming. More accentuation will be put on marking that gives point by point data about the healthful substance and elements of items, permitting purchasers to settle on informed decisions. The food business will keep on creating utilitarian food varieties and dietary enhancements that address explicit wellbeing concerns, and customized sustenance might turn out to be more open as innovation progresses.

The fate of Homestead to Fork will likewise include a change by they way we view food as medication. Wellbeing experts and policymakers are perceiving the significance of an eating regimen wealthy in natural products, vegetables, and entire grains to forestall and oversee ongoing illnesses. Later on, medical services suppliers might recommend customized dietary plans and team up with ranchers and food makers to guarantee admittance to new, nutritious food sources for patients. This approach could assist with decreasing medical care costs and further develop general wellbeing results.

The significance of sanitation will stay a foundation representing things to come of Homestead to Fork. With the globalization of the food inventory network, the gamble of foodborne diseases and pollution stays a huge concern. Severe food handling guidelines and assessments will keep on being fundamental to safeguard general wellbeing. Arising advances, as referenced prior, will add to quicker discovery and control of foodborne microorganisms, improving the security of the food supply.

Besides, the eventual fate of Ranch to Fork will include tending to the social and financial parts of food creation and conveyance. A more fair and comprehensive food framework will be vital, guaranteeing that all people approach nutritious and reasonable food. This incorporates resolving issues of food deserts and food frailty, where low-pay networks need admittance to new, quality food choices. Drives to help nearby and limited scope ranchers, as well as fair exchange and moral obtaining rehearses, will acquire unmistakable quality.

Later on, there will likewise be a push for more noteworthy straightforwardness in food naming, for example, uncovering the circumstances in which creatures are raised, the utilization of hereditarily changed organic entities (GMOs), and the natural effect of food items. Shoppers will approach more data about the social and moral acts of the organizations behind the items they purchase.

This expanded straightforwardness will engage buyers to pursue decisions that line up with their qualities, whether those values are connected with creature government assistance, natural maintainability, or fair work rehearses.

The eventual fate of Homestead to Fork will require cooperative endeavors from all partners in the food framework. State run administrations, organizations, non-legislative associations, and customers should cooperate to accomplish the ideal results. Government strategies and impetuses will assume a urgent part in forming the eventual fate of food frameworks. Appropriations and guidelines can support maintainable cultivating rehearses, the decrease of food squander, and the advancement of smart dieting. Public-private organizations can drive advancement and interest in maintainable horticulture, sanitation, and food innovation. Common society associations and shopper backing gatherings will keep on bringing issues to light and promoter for change.

9.1 Trends and innovations in the food industry

The food business is continually advancing to meet the changing requirements and inclinations of buyers, as well as to address worldwide difficulties like food security, supportability, and wellbeing. In this time of fast mechanical progression and expanding attention to the natural and wellbeing effects of our food decisions, a few critical patterns and developments are forming the fate of the food business.

Perhaps of the most conspicuous pattern in the food business is the developing interest for plant-based and elective protein items. Purchasers are progressively searching out plant-based choices, for example, meat substitutes produced using fixings like soy, pea protein, and mycoprotein. This pattern is driven by worries over wellbeing, ecological manageability, and creature government assistance. Plant-based slims down are seen as better, as they are in many cases lower in soaked fats and cholesterol. Besides, they have a decreased ecological impression, as they require less normal assets, like water and land, and produce less ozone harming substance outflows contrasted with conventional domesticated animals cultivating. The ascent of elective protein sources is changing the business, with organizations like Past Meat and Inconceivable Food sources acquiring standard fame. This pattern isn't restricted to meat substitutes; plant-based dairy options, like almond, soy, and oat milk, have additionally acquired critical piece of the pie.

One more critical pattern in the food business is the attention on manageability and ecological obligation. Customers are progressively worried about the natural effect of their food decisions, from creation to removal. This has prompted an ascent in manageable practices and confirmations in the food area. Organizations are doing whatever it takes to decrease squander, moderate assets, and lower their carbon impression. Drives incorporate diminishing single-use plastics, executing energy-proficient creation processes, and embracing bundling arrangements that are more eco-accommodating.

Supportable obtaining of fixings and straightforward stock chains are likewise becoming fundamental for buyers who need to go with informed decisions. Additionally, roundabout economy standards are building up some decent momentum, with endeavors to diminish food squander and reuse food results and waste into new items or energy sources.

Innovation and development are driving huge changes in the food business. Progresses in biotechnology, like hereditary designing and quality altering, are reshaping the manner in which we produce and devour food. Hereditarily changed organic entities (GMOs) have been a subject of contention, yet they have likewise assumed a urgent part in expanding crop yields and decreasing the requirement for substance pesticides. All the more as of late, quality altering strategies like CRISPR-Cas9 can possibly make crops with upgraded nourishing profiles, protection from infections, and worked on ecological flexibility. Nonetheless, the acknowledgment and guideline of these advancements remain subjects of discussion, with worries about potentially negative side-effects and moral ramifications.

Man-made brainpower (artificial intelligence) and information examination are additionally changing the food business. These innovations empower better inventory network the board, customized nourishment proposals, and further developed sanitation measures. Man-made intelligence driven calculations can improve creation processes, diminish squander, and foresee market request all the more precisely. Additionally, blockchain innovation is being utilized to build straightforwardness and discernibility in the food production network, guaranteeing that shoppers approach precise data about the beginning and nature of their food. This can help in instances of food reviews and in building trust among purchasers and food makers.

3D printing is one more imaginative innovation with applications in the food business. It considers the making of complicated and tweaked food items, going from chocolates to complex sugar models. 3D food printing can possibly change food customization, especially in medical services, where custom-made sustenance and dietary limitations can be met all the more actually. It likewise opens up additional opportunities for gourmet experts and food planners to make outwardly dazzling and interesting culinary encounters.

The ascent of internet business and online food conveyance stages significantly affects the food business. With the accommodation of requesting food from the solace of one's home, purchasers are progressively going to online stages to fulfill their culinary cravings. This pattern has prompted the fast development of food conveyance administrations, like Uber Eats, GrubHub, and DoorDash. Also, direct-to-shopper food conveyance models, especially for feast packs and specialty items, have acquired notoriety. Purchasers can now get to a more extensive assortment of food varieties and cooking styles, including global choices that might not have been promptly accessible in their neighborhood markets.

The food business is likewise seeing a change in buyer inclinations towards clean name and normal food sources. Clean mark items are portrayed by less complex fixing records with conspicuous and normal fixings.

This pattern is driven by a craving for straightforwardness and the evasion of fake added substances and additives. Shoppers are progressively searching for food sources that are liberated from fake tones, flavors, and additives. This inclination for clean name items has prompted a resurgence of interest in conventional and high quality food readiness techniques, like maturation, relieving, and pickling, which are viewed as more normal and bona fide.

Personalization in the food business is another arising pattern. As customers become more wellbeing cognizant and mindful of their dietary requirements, there is a developing interest for customized nourishment plans and items. Customized sustenance can be custom-made to a singular's particular dietary necessities, sensitivities, and wellbeing objectives. Organizations are utilizing simulated intelligence and information investigation to give customized dietary suggestions, and some are in any event, offering redid food items in light of a person's hereditary profile. This pattern lines up with the more extensive development towards preventive medical care and an emphasis on health through diet.

Sanitation and detectability keep on being foremost worries in the food business. The capacity to follow the beginning of food items and guarantee their wellbeing is fundamental for customer certainty and general wellbeing. Propels in innovation, for example, blockchain and DNA barcoding, are making it simpler to follow the excursion of food from ranch to fork. These devices empower fast distinguishing proof of foodborne microorganisms, diminishing the gamble of foodborne ailments. Moreover, severe guidelines and global principles are set up to guarantee the wellbeing and nature of food items.

The pattern of globalization is additionally affecting the food business. Customers approach a more extensive assortment of worldwide cooking styles and fixings, which has prompted an expanded interest for fascinating and different food sources. This pattern has extended the market for ethnic and specialty food varieties, as well as set out open doors for food organizations to investigate new culinary combinations and flavors. Culturally diverse food encounters and combination cooking are on the ascent as gourmet experts and food business people explore different avenues regarding the mixing of various culinary practices.

Besides, the food business is encountering changes in customer assumptions about moral and social obligation. Shoppers are progressively searching for brands and items that line up with their qualities, whether it's connected with creature government assistance, fair work practices, or local area commitment. Organizations are feeling the squeeze to take on additional moral and maintainable practices, and those that neglect to do so gamble with confronting purchaser kickback and reputational harm.

The food business is likewise answering the requirement for decreased food squander. Food squander is a worldwide issue with critical monetary and natural outcomes. Advancements in food protection, bundling, and dissemination are assisting with broadening the timeframe of realistic usability of food items and lessen decay.

Furthermore, drives to reuse food squander into esteem added items or give overflow food to those in need are turning out to be more boundless.

The fate of the food business is a unique scene molded by these patterns and developments. Shoppers will keep on driving change, requesting better, more maintainable, and morally created food. Innovation will assume a focal part in molding how food is delivered, conveyed, and ate. As the world countenances complex difficulties connected with populace development, environmental change, and asset shortage, the food business will be at the cutting edge of endeavors to foster arrangements that guarantee an economical and strong food supply for a long time into the future.

9.2 Challenges and opportunities for the future

What's to come presents a horde of difficulties and valuable open doors across different spaces, from innovation and medical services to financial matters and the climate. As we explore the intricacies of an always impacting world, it's fundamental to recognize and address these difficulties while saddling the potential open doors they offer. In this conversation, we will investigate the absolute most squeezing difficulties and energizing possibilities for what's in store.

1. **Environmental Change and Natural Manageability:**
   Perhaps of the most pressing test we face is environmental change. Increasing temperatures, outrageous climate occasions, and the deficiency of biodiversity are ramifications of our evolving environment. To relieve and adjust to these difficulties, we should change to a low-carbon economy, decrease ozone harming substance outflows, and safeguard fundamental biological systems. The open door here is to foster inventive innovations, feasible practices, and green framework that can resolve these issues while making new positions and monetary open doors.

2. **Medical care and Pandemic Readiness:**
   The continuous Coronavirus pandemic has featured the requirement for hearty medical services frameworks and pandemic readiness. Challenges incorporate guaranteeing impartial admittance to medical services, further developing medical care framework, and tending to the psychological wellness effects of the pandemic. The open door lies in utilizing telemedicine and computerized well-being advancements to upgrade medical care access and further develop illness reconnaissance, early discovery, and therapy.

3. **Innovative Progressions:**
   Fast mechanical progressions, especially in man-made brainpower (computer based intelligence), biotechnology, and sustainable power, offer various open doors and difficulties. The improvement of computer based intelligence can possibly change businesses, yet it additionally brings up moral issues about information protection, inclination, and the effect on work.
   Biotechnology holds guarantee in relieving sicknesses, yet it presents situations

connected with hereditary altering, cloning, and biosecurity. Environmentally friendly power offers a feasible option in contrast to petroleum products, yet the test is to speed up its reception and put resources into foundation and exploration to make it more proficient and practical.

4. **Financial Disparity:**

Financial disparity keeps on being a huge worldwide test. The Coronavirus pandemic exacerbated differences in pay, admittance to training, and medical care. As we plan ahead, it's fundamental for address these disparities through moderate tax collection, social security nets, and instruction and occupation preparing programs. A comprehensive and evenhanded economy can prompt expanded development and efficiency, helping society overall.

5. **Online protection and Information Security:**

The advanced age has brought unrivaled availability and comfort, however it has likewise presented us to huge network protection chances. The test is to shield delicate information and basic foundation from cyberattacks while regarding individual security. Open doors lie in the improvement of vigorous network protection measures, including encryption, multifaceted validation, and simulated intelligence driven danger location, as well as more grounded information security guidelines to shield individual data.

6. **Segment Moves and Maturing Populaces:**

Numerous locales all over the planet are encountering segment shifts, with maturing populaces turning out to be more predominant. Challenges related with this shift incorporate expanded medical services costs, annuity maintainability, and giving sufficient consideration to the old. Notwithstanding, there are potential chances to make age-accommodating networks, foster advances to help free living, and saddle the experience and shrewdness of more established people in the labor force.

7. **Instruction and Long lasting Learning:**

The future will expect people to adjust and get new abilities all through their lives to stay serious in the gig market. This presents a test regarding admittance to quality schooling and retraining open doors. The open door lies in growing web based learning stages, professional preparation programs, and deep rooted learning drives that engage people to secure new abilities and remain pertinent in a quickly changing position scene.

8. **Food Security and Agribusiness:**

Taking care of a developing worldwide populace economically is a test that should be tended to even with environmental change, asset shortage, and food squander. What's in store offers valuable chances to embrace regenerative agrarian practices, foster dry season safe yields, and advance feasible food frameworks. Accuracy horticulture, vertical cultivating, and elective protein sources additionally present creative answers for these difficulties.

9. **Emotional wellness and Prosperity:**
   The requests and stresses of present day life, exacerbated by the pandemic, have carried emotional well-being and prosperity to the very front. The test is to decrease the shame encompassing emotional wellness, further develop admittance to mental medical care, and establish steady conditions. What's in store offers open doors for the improvement of psychological well-being applications, teletherapy, and local area based emotional wellness programs that can offer fundamental help.

10. **Worldwide Administration and Collaboration:**
    As we face progressively interconnected worldwide difficulties, successful global collaboration is crucial. Challenges incorporate political pressures, protectionist arrangements, and the requirement for worked on worldwide administration. The open door is to fortify worldwide establishments, produce collusions to address worldwide emergencies, and advance tact and collaboration despite shared difficulties like environmental change, pandemics, and clashes.

11. **Energy Change and Supportable Foundation:**
    Progressing to economical energy sources is essential for lessening fossil fuel byproducts and fighting environmental change. Challenges incorporate the progress costs, framework necessities, and the requirement for political will to help these changes. Open doors are plentiful in creating environmentally friendly power advances, building supportable framework, and making green positions that can animate financial development while lessening our carbon impression.

12. **Space Investigation and Mechanical Development:**
    The eventual fate of room investigation presents a great many difficulties and potential open doors. Challenges incorporate the immense distances and intricacies of room travel, as well as moral contemplations in regards to space garbage and expected extraterrestrial life. Open doors lie in logical revelations, mechanical progressions, and the potential for space colonization, which could open up new outskirts for humankind and drive advancement on The planet.

13. **Social and Racial Value:**
    Accomplishing social and racial value is a huge test in many regions of the planet. What's in store offers chances to address foundational imbalances through strategy changes, hostile to separation measures, and civil rights drives. Comprehensive and different social orders can outfit the maximum capacity of their populaces, encouraging imagination and development.

14. **Water Shortage and Asset The board:**

Water shortage is a squeezing worldwide issue, exacerbated by environmental change and impractical asset the executives. Challenges incorporate guaranteeing fair admittance to clean water, safeguarding freshwater environments, and saving this fundamental asset. Potential open doors emerge from embracing water-effective advancements, creating water reusing frameworks, and executing feasible water the board rehearses.

9.3 The role of consumers in shaping the food evolution

The food business is in a condition of steady development, driven by a huge number of elements, however quite possibly of the main power forming the fate of food is the job of purchasers. As shoppers become more educated, wellbeing cognizant, and naturally mindful, they use impressive impact over what winds up on their plates and how it's created. In this conversation, we will dive into the multi-layered job customers play in forming the food scene.

1. **Changing Dietary Inclinations:**

   Shoppers assume a crucial part in molding food development through their dietary inclinations. As individuals become more wellbeing cognizant, there is a developing interest for better food choices. This incorporates an inclination for entire food varieties, natural products, vegetables, lean proteins, and diminished utilization of profoundly handled and sweet food varieties. The "perfect eating" development, for instance, has built up momentum as customers search out food sources with straightforward, normal fixings and less added substances.

   Furthermore, changing dietary inclinations incorporate the ascent of vegetarianism and veganism. A developing number of customers are taking on plant-based consumes less calories for wellbeing, natural, and moral reasons. This shift has prompted a blast of plant-based items, including meat substitutes, dairy choices, and veggie lover well disposed bundled food sources. The interest for plant-based choices isn't just affecting item accessibility yet additionally driving advancements in food innovation to make reasonable and tasty plant-based other options.

2. **Manageability and Moral Contemplations:**

   Customers are progressively worried about the ecological and moral effect of their food decisions. This has prompted an interest for supportable and morally obtained items. Shoppers are searching for food that is created with insignificant damage to the climate, including decreased ozone harming substance outflows, dependable land use, and restricted water utilization. Maintainable fish decisions and guaranteed natural items are only a couple of instances of this pattern.

   Moral contemplations additionally stretch out to creature government assistance. As customers become more mindful of the circumstances wherein creatures are raised for food, they are pushing for more others conscious treatment. This has prompted an interest for items marked as "confine free," "free roaming," and "grass-took care of." Moreover, there is developing interest in options to conventional animal cultivating, for example, lab-developed meat and bug based protein, which can possibly lessen creature enduring and bring down the natural impression of food creation.

3. **Straightforwardness and Food Marking:**

Shoppers are progressively looking for straightforwardness in the food they purchase. They need to know where their food comes from, how it's delivered, and what it contains. Food marking has turned into a basic device for giving this data. Marks like "non-GMO," "natural," and "fair exchange" are fundamental for buyers pursuing informed decisions about the items they buy.

Besides, there is a developing interest for clear and succinct nourishment marks. Purchasers need to know the wholesome substance of the items they purchase, remembering data for calories, fats, sugars, and fixings. This has prompted unofficial laws commanding more nitty gritty and educational nourishment marking on food bundling. Organizations that embrace straightforward marking can fabricate entrust with purchasers and gain an upper hand.

4. **Neighborhood and Feasible Obtaining:**

The "ranch to-table" or "locavore" development mirrors shoppers' craving to help neighborhood and supportable food frameworks. Numerous customers are enthused about purchasing food delivered nearer to home, supporting neighborhood ranchers, and decreasing the carbon impression related with significant distance food transportation. This pattern has driven the development of ranchers' business sectors, local area upheld farming (CSA) projects, and neighborhood food cooperatives.

Feasible obtaining is likewise a basic thought for customers. They need to realize that the food they eat is developed and gathered in a way that saves the climate and advantages neighborhood networks. Organizations that focus on nearby and maintainable obtaining line up with purchaser values as well as add to the improvement of strong and harmless to the ecosystem food frameworks.

5. **Food Squander Decrease:**

Customers are progressively mindful of the issue of food squander and are doing whatever it takes to lessen it. This incorporates more effective feast arranging, better capacity of food, and lessening parts to stay away from extras. There's likewise a developing appreciation for "terrible" produce, which probably won't fulfill the severe restorative guidelines of the business however is completely great to eat. Supporting drives to divert surplus food to those out of luck, for example, food banks and food salvage programs, is another way purchasers are handling food squander.

Organizations are likewise answering this pattern by offering items and administrations pointed toward decreasing food squander. For example, there are applications that assist customers with arranging dinners in view of what they as of now have at home and administrations that convey defective or excess produce to buyers at a markdown.

6. **Interest for Accommodation and Online Food Conveyance:**

   In our speedy world, comfort is a critical driver of shopper decisions. The interest for fast and simple dinners has prompted the development of the food conveyance industry. Organizations like Uber Eats, DoorDash, and GrubHub offer customers the comfort of requesting food from many cafés and cooking styles, all conveyed to their doorstep. This pattern has reshaped the café business and the manner in which individuals contemplate feasting out.

   Moreover, feast unit conveyance administrations have become progressively famous. These administrations furnish purchasers with pre-distributed fixings and recipes for planning feasts at home, diminishing food waste and offering comfort. The eventual fate of food conveyance and feast units will probably include advancements in manageable bundling, sustenance customization, and further developing the general client experience.

7. **Wellbeing and Health Applications:**

   The expansion of cell phones and wearable gadgets has prompted the advancement of wellbeing and health applications that enable customers to settle on informed food decisions. These applications offer elements like calorie following, nourishing examination, recipe ideas, and, surprisingly, customized diet plans in view of individual wellbeing objectives and dietary inclinations.

   Wellbeing and health applications furnish shoppers with significant data as well as advance responsibility and good dieting propensities. As innovation keeps on propelling, these applications will turn out to be progressively complex, offering more thorough and customized direction.

8. **Local area Commitment and Food Developments:**

   Buyers are effectively captivating with their nearby networks and taking part in food developments. Local area gardens, food centers, and neighborhood cooking clubs are instances of how buyers are meeting up to find out about, develop, and share food. These exercises advance a feeling of local area, instruction, and food independence.

   Food developments, for example, the sluggish food development, center around protecting culinary customs, supporting nearby food frameworks, and pushing for earth manageable and moral food rehearses. These developments are driven by purchaser values and longings for more significant and capable food decisions.

9. **Effect of Online Entertainment and Food Forces to be reckoned with:**

Web-based entertainment stages play had a critical impact in forming buyer food inclinations. Food powerhouses and bloggers have acquired significant followings, and their supports can influence food patterns and decisions. Purchasers are presented to a wide cluster of culinary encounters, from outlandish cooking styles to stylish weight control plans, and are impacted by the visual and tactile allure of food pictures and recordings.

Virtual entertainment can both intensify attention to significant food-related issues and cultivate unfortunate food patterns. Thus, it is fundamental for buyers to basically assess the data they experience and settle on informed decisions in light of their qualities and dietary requirements.